Mysticism and Modern Life:

Ancient Wisdom for Personal Growth

Mysticism and Modern Life:

Ancient Wisdom for Personal Growth

Larry Laveman

Dedicated to Gregge Tiffen,
esteemed mystic and mentor.

CONTENTS

Note from the Author

The inspiration for writing *Mysticism and Modern Life* comes from my interest in holism. As far back as I can remember, I wanted to reach beyond the boundaries of common life and grasp what was on the other side. I did not have a fascination with the supernatural or the occult, but I did carry a healthy skepticism about my formal education. No matter how I rationalized it, I could not reconcile my life experience with what I was learning in school. The discrepancy between my experience and education intensified when I was sixteen years old and had my first psychic dream.

On June 5, 1968, I fell asleep while waiting for Bobby Kennedy to make his victory speech in the California primary. I dreamed I was walking with my girlfriend through a cemetery looking at all the headstones, but could not make out any of the names. I awoke just as Kennedy was leaving the podium and watched in horror as Sirhan Sirhan assassinated him. I kept that dream to myself for quite a while as it frightened me. It marked the beginning of my investigation into the polarities of the mystical and the mundane, an inquiry lasting for the next ten years.

The first outlet I found for my nontraditional beliefs occurred while reading *A Yaqui Way of Knowledge* by Carlos Castaneda in 1970. Castaneda, a reclusive UCLA anthropology student who went on to write twelve books about his apprenticeship with the Mexican shaman don Juan Matus, encouraged a generation of readers to see the life force in all things. The controversy over the veracity of Castaneda's accounts of his training with don Juan still exists today. Was he reporting from his field notes or was he writing fiction? Even during my college days, the legitimacy of his claims was irrelevant to me. I was more taken with his alternative model of reality than with its factual basis. Since I already believed reality extended beyond the range of our physical senses, I found Castaneda's world of sorcery powerful, provocative, and irresistible. The sharp contrast between the formulaic pretensions of my conventional education and Castaneda's magical world was another glimpse into the raw strength and creative power of polarities.

My metaphysical speculation became even stronger in graduate school after reading Carl Jung's (1961) memoirs. I was particularly struck by his chapter entitled "Visions," in which he describes his 1944 near-death experience following his heart attack.

Caught in the space between life and death in the moments after his heart attack, Jung experienced the joy of being released from the containment of his physical body, while back on earth he was given oxygen and camphor injections to help stabilize him. In his euphoria he floated high above the planet in full contentment. Having shed all of his prior regrets and feeling free of pain and restriction, he encountered the ethereal form of his doctor who told him about a protest on earth "against his death." At that point, Jung's vision stopped, his pulse stabilized, and he regained consciousness.

Three weeks of depression follow his revival, as Jung came to terms with what he called the *box system* of physical life. He had to convince himself that the restriction of living in a human box was important. Jung, who spent his entire life charting a systematic course to help people expand the confines of humanity, found that no matter how hard he tried, he could not escape the containment of the physical body.

This particular recollection of Jung's life and Castaneda's paranormal experiences in the Sonoran desert were so consistent with my interest in life's larger contexts, it spurred me into gestalt therapy, energy transference, and philosophy.

My early professional work culminated in 1977 when my dear friend and early mentor, Barbra Dillenger, introduced me to Gregge Tiffen. Gregge, a Tibetan-trained mystic, became to me what don Juan was to Castaneda. Under his tutelage, I learned the mechanics of metaphysics. Integral to his teaching was the relationship between the polarities of the macrocosm and the microcosm.

Simply put, the microcosm is born out of the macrocosm, giving both the same patterning and structure. The microcosm, therefore, becomes the representative of the larger whole of the macrocosm. This basic understanding of the relationship between the macrocosm and the microcosm helped me to reconcile the polar split I was experiencing between the mystical world of my Kennedy dream and the mundane world around me.

I began to see the sensitivity some people have to nonphysical forces—experiences such as clairvoyance, prescience, and the paranormal—as one way of connecting to a larger context beyond the range of our physical senses. I came to understand Jung's "full contentment" experience could only happen after he shed the physical constraints of his body and could connect to a larger context. Within this larger context, Jung gained spiritual insight into the box system of human life and caught a glimpse of the interaction between the macrocosm and the microcosm he wrote about so prolifically.

With Barbra and Gregge's help, I developed a metaphysical framework, adding an extra dimension to my life without discounting life's ordinary qualities. In the ensuing years, I have not disregarded my normal life for a spiritual quest or ignored everything I learned in school. Instead I have combined the qualities of the mystical and the mundane into one coherent system in, *Mysticism and Modern Life.*

In the book, I present a framework for viewing life within the larger contexts I have struggled to define since childhood. In presenting the part to whole philosophy of mysticism, I draw from case examples, as well as from literary works of Musil, Canetti, Borges, Tan, and Mann; the philosophy of Kierkegaard, Wilber, Emerson, Heraclitus, and Plato; the Jewish mysticism of Steinsaltz and Heschel; the psychology of Freud, Jung, Winnicott, Becker, and a host of post Freudians; the poetry of Frost, Blake, and Neruda, and; the social science of Bateson, von Bertalanffy, and Levi-Strauss. I include many knowledgeable voices in the text since the concepts are universal. In other words, they are found in different historical eras, domains of life, and modes of expression such as poetry, literature, philosophy, and psychology.

By distilling the concept of mysticism down to six principles I show readers how human life and universal principles correspond to each other and how our lives are actually part of a larger organizing scheme.

I focus on a predominant universal principle—the law of polarity. I particularly rely upon the Greek philosopher Heraclitus, who was one of the first philosophers to show that polarities were the by-products of unity. By seeing human beings as a meeting place for various levels of reality, he created a multidimensional philosophy of human existence demonstrating the connection between the unity of the cosmos and diversity of its people.

Due to the verbal tradition of ancient sages handing down information to their students, we have only sixty fragments scholars can attribute to Heraclitus (Geldard, 2000). By referring to the ancient teachings of Heraclitus within the flow of the book and in the epigraphs, I try to create a sense of continuity and clarify the correspondence between mystical principles and human development.

Finally, I hope this book will reveal to readers, if only incrementally, how a small individual expression, unique and complete within itself, can have a positive influence on the world.

Larry Laveman
Solana Beach, California
June 2006

Foreword

Mysticism is everywhere. It is the connection each of us feels to something much greater than ourselves. It is in the unexplainable coincidences happening so often in life, in the clairvoyance we possess, and in the deep state of reverence we feel when a loved one passes away. It is in the big and small things, the complex and simple things, and in the obvious and subtle things. Every now and then, we catch glimpses of our connections to the mystical. But for the most part, we live day to day without any awareness of our part in a larger organizing scheme.

Mysticism and Modern Life shows how our lives exist within ever-widening patterns of relationships that connect us to something much greater than ourselves. By becoming conscious of our personal patterns within the context of larger patterns, we will develop stronger connections to ourselves and to the humanity we share.

The book focuses on how we can achieve higher levels of personality development by integrating ancient principles with developmental theory. With this information, readers can appreciate how the smallest behavior carries enormous implications when placed within a larger context. No life, and consequently no action, is insignificant when seen as an expression of something much greater than ourselves. Instead of giving ourselves to a greater cause, I maintain we are part of a greater cause. We are challenged to preserve our unique identities as we engage others to create bigger and better contexts.

Mysticism and Modern Life is divided into three sections. The first section lays the foundation for the correspondence between mystical principles and everyday life by identifying six principles of mysticism, the law of polarity being the third principle, and examining how mysticism and modern life relate to each other within the context of these principles.

The second section highlights the law of polarity in personality development, choice of mate, and the development of repetitive patterns of behavior so readers can see the interplay between mysticism and modern life. In this section, I present some practical exercises for developing a conscious marriage, along with specific examples showing how to apply these principles.

By the end of the book, readers learn how, by extending beyond the constraints of family of origin influences, transcendence is used in a practical way to develop a *true self*. Readers begin to understand the etiology of personality constraints, how to identify them, and how to move beyond them to reach higher levels of personality development. Thus, the true self unfolds.

Recognizing that people other than our parents raised many of us, I refer to all significant early childhood caregivers as parents. Throughout the book, the term *identity* conveys the sense of *who I am* and not merely the separate existence from another person. Since gender forms have been challenging to writers for the past decade, I use both the male and female forms for parity. The use of the term marriage can apply to any significant relationship where two people share their lives together.

Each chapter ends with a detailed summary. Readers can return to the summaries to clarify basic concepts or refresh their memories of major points.

Section One: Mysticism and Society

Chapter One: An Introduction to Mysticism and Modern Life

Listening to the Logos and not to me, it is wise to agree that all things are one.

Heraclitus

In February 1996, my father had a heart attack while playing golf with my mother in Myrtle Beach. As it was off-season, the course was completely empty and my mother panicked.

Nearby, a woman was trying to free her car from deep mud when she heard my mother's frantic cries for help. Racing from her car through the woods, she came upon my poor mother and instantly took charge.

She was a nurse; her name was Angelina. She gave my father CPR, eventually reviving him, while my mother drove to the clubhouse to call for an ambulance.

My father died four hours later at the local hospital. My mother knew everything humanly possible was done to save his life. Angelina, known in our family as the *Angel from the Woods,* rescued my mother more than my father. My father could not be saved, but my mother was spared the guilt of thinking if she only knew CPR, she could have prevented his death.

Several weeks later, I asked my mom what she would have done if Angelina had not appeared. She hesitated for a minute, then realized the full implications of Angelina's appearance.

During our most desperate moments, we each encounter our own Angel from the Woods. Such synchronistic events are the portals to mysticism. Angelina arrived on the scene like a messenger from God. The timing of her appearance was nothing short of miraculous. It was as if she and my mother shared an invisible bond with each other, a bond that Hillman (1996) says is most apparent at moments of exaggerated importance. At these times, things magically fall into place; connecting us to each other like links in a chain. Within this interconnection, we find the roots of mysticism.

Mysticism refers to entering into the mystery of life and finding a deeper connection with the underlying forces of everyday experiences. Taken from the Greek word *mystikos*, it means "entering into mystery." Although I have rational ways of explaining the appearance of Angelina at the time of my father's heart attack, at a deeper level, I cannot explain it at all.

Mysticism is not only mysterious, it's ineffable. While we can speak of mysticism we can never quantify it. It is beyond words, beyond description, and beyond our comprehension. Yet the principles of mysticism are with us all the time, connecting our mundane world to the hidden mysteries of the universe.

Mysticism relates us to a larger reality. It is within us, making us representatives of the overall mystical structure. In the mystical tradition, everything is connected to everything else, producing an overall web of interaction.

The Foundation of Mysticism

The Great Leap of Being: The emergence of mysticism can be traced to the period from 500 BC – 250 BC, in what historian Erik Voegelin (1957) calls the "Great Leap of Being" and the German philosopher Karl Jaspers (1951) refers to as the "Axial Age." It was a time of questioning and self-examination. Ideas put forth in the sacred Hindu text, the *Upanishads,* and by such great teachers as Confucius, Lao-tzu, Buddha, Pythagoras, Heraclitus, and Plato, who independently proposed an Ultimate Reality from which all things emanate. Prior to this time, the prevailing cultural myth focused on worshipping godlike figures that stood separate from the rest of humanity. With the rise of mysticism, the consciousness shifted from trying to please the gods to investigating the relationship between people and a singular god.

From these early roots, comes the philosophy of a singular source of life connecting everything to everything else. Support for the singular source is found in all religious and mystical systems throughout history. In *The Varieties of Religious Experience,* William James stated there was an "eternal unanimity" about the existence of an absolute order. We may call the singular source God, the One, Divine Consciousness, Ultimate Reality, Brahman, Allah, or the Holy Other. Or we may refer to the singular source in Sufism, Buddhism, Judaism, or Christian mysticism. Regardless, the idea of an underlying unity to life remains constant.

As we ponder this information, two logical questions arise: How do we get a diverse population from a singular source? What is our connection to that source?

Exploring the answers to these questions, we see the reciprocal connection between the mystical and the mundane. First, however, to establish a clear definition of mysticism, we must address some important distinctions between *mysticism*, *mystical states*, and *transcendence*.

Defining Mysticism and Transcendence

Mysticism is a way of thinking, a philosophy explaining how large and small forces are the expression of a singular universal source. A mystical state is the sense of oneness we experience when we tap into that source. With its emphasis on fulfillment, completion, balance, and harmony, a mystical state of unity is an ideal form we try to emulate. Its positive characteristics provide hope of rising above our imperfect human nature to a place of beauty and bliss.

Transcendence is the movement beyond the constraints we inherit or impose upon ourselves, into new and freer ways of behaving. In this regard, transcendence on the physical plane is homologous to the mystical concept of transcendence. Both actions move people beyond their restrictions toward a more complete experience of harmony and wholeness. Transcendence is prominent as we explore different ways of reaching higher levels of personality development.

As we attempt a mystical connection with the singular source, a curious contradiction occurs—we find that we are both connected to the singular source, yet remain separate and distinct at the same time. This is known as the *central paradox of mysticism*. Although we can experience unity during prayer, deep meditation, or peak experiences, we always return to who we are. We simply cannot get away from ourselves and our own physical nature. No matter how hard we try to transcend our physical limitations, our attempts to achieve true mystical harmony deliver us right back to our individual identities. Although our hope for transcendence never fails, our attempts to achieve it are hindered.

According to Huston Smith, the esteemed philosopher and religious scholar, we should not try to transcend our physical nature for the attainment of an undifferentiated unity with the singular source because such efforts make our commitment to the physical world more difficult. Quoting a Hindu devotional classic in his venerable book *The World's Religions* (1958), Smith reiterates, "I want to taste sugar: I don't want to be sugar." As physical beings our lessons are learned with our feet on the ground—which is not to devalue awareness, insight, mental discipline, or other forms of therapy in the pursuit of greater balance and harmony—just not at the expense of learning how to resolve life's problems by elevating above them.

Mysticism and human life are not separate experiences, but related experiences, just as good and bad are related experiences. Rather than view events as random or disconnected, we realize all events are part of a larger web of connection. Crucial to understanding our connection to mysticism is a more detailed exploration of its central paradox.

Understanding the Central Paradox of Mysticism

At its core, the central paradox demonstrates the singular and dualistic nature of mysticism. In its singular form, mysticism is a complete sense of oneness. The example of Jung's near death experience in the "Note from the Author," exemplifies this state of unity. In its dualistic form, mysticism refers to the world of restrictions we live in, the one Jung found so depressing after his heart attack. The paradox is that we cannot live in a singular and dualistic world at the same time, yet both worlds effect us directly and simultaneously.

We may believe the merger of the soul with the singular source is the goal of life, as in some Eastern religions. Or in the Judaic-Christian religion, where we believe we can seek knowledge of, but not ultimate union with, the singular source. Regardless of belief, in the end, human life depends upon our remaining separate from the unity we consider and can rarely experience.

Lao-tzu's philosophy: Our inability to live on two levels of reality led ancient mystics to use paradoxes, poetics, and symbols to shake the rational mind free of limitations and achieve a mystical union with a nondual reality. Lao-tzu, the great Chinese philosopher who founded

Taoism, wrote his philosophy in the *Tao-te Ching*. In poetic prose punctuated with paradoxes, he speaks of this dilemma in his opening verse:

> *The Tao that can be followed is not the eternal Tao.*
> *The name that can be named is not the eternal name.*

In these two lines, he addresses the central paradox of mysticism: unity, the mystical sense of oneness, transforms into a duality once it is translated into human experience. *The name that can be named is not the eternal name* because once you name *the eternal* you reduce it to description, which means you have lost its essence. Speaking in negatives, Lao-tzu employed a mechanism common to many ancient mystics. By using contradictory and incongruous terms and negation, he tried to bend his students' minds from dualism toward enlightenment.

The mysticism of Lao-tzu is twofold: his ability to perceive wholeness and his way of bringing wholeness into the mundane world. With calculating authority, he expanded his students' minds into ever-widening circles, until they realized they were both the circle and the arc at the same time.

Carlos Castaneda's contribution: The interplay of the mystical and the mundane is found in the contemporary stories of Carlos Castaneda. As an apprentice to the sorcerer don Juan Matus, Castaneda went through a transformation from his highbrow skepticism of the extrasensory world to a profound reverence for the unseen forces shaping reality.

Similar to Lao-tzu, don Juan provokes Castaneda by challenging his assumptions with techniques designed to confuse and confound him. While casually talking, don Juan grabbed his young student's attention with a loud noise, convulsive laughter, or a sudden movement. The abrupt behavior shattered Castaneda's rationality, exposing him to a deeper and completely unexpected level of reality. With two realities to consider, Castaneda wondered if his prior worldview was a figment of his imagination, or if he was lost in a mystical haze compliments of the sorcerer don Juan.

As Castaneda's cultural odyssey unfolds from one book to the next, we see that don Juan was not a separatist, but an integrationist. He showed Castaneda how two worlds of reality exist simultaneously; one in a real and physical sense and one when we suspend our rationality. As don Juan liked to say, we must learn how to "stop the world" and allow ourselves to consider the larger context underlying everyday events.

From Lao-tzu to Castaneda, the central paradox of mysticism describes two simultaneous levels of reality—the singular source and the physical world of dualities. Through this mystical context our physical life does not exist separate from its connection to the larger whole, since the singular source is the ground of all existence.

Getting a Diverse Population from a Singular Source

The answer to the question posed earlier, How do we get a diverse population from a singular source? becomes clear as we define the concepts of *awareness*, *karma*, and the *law of polarity* in their mystical context.

Awareness—the singular source focuses on itself: In its original state, the singular source is nondual; it exists as an undifferentiated state of bliss with no awareness of itself. The dualistic world—our world of polarities—exists when the singular source focuses on itself, thereby bringing awareness of itself into the world.

Founder of the neo-Platonic movement, Plotinus proposed that by virtue of knowing it exists, the singular source also knows it is no longer singular. It is the subject of its own inquiry, creating a subject and an object, or a duality.

Awareness, the ability of anything to reflect upon itself, is the first emanation of mysticism since it produces its own form of expansion by creating diversity. Without awareness we are reduced to instinct, essential for our survival, but not adequate enough to advance the human race. When we use awareness to contemplate our lives, understand the motivations for our actions, delve into the unconscious, and plan the future, we are initiating acts of expansion parallel to the mystical theory of existence. In modern philosophy, the clear perception of subject/object duality led Descartes to exclaim, "I think, therefore I am."

Karma—the relationship between cause and effect: In mysticism, all polarities stem from the initial act of contemplation that gives the singular source an awareness of itself. If awareness is the first emanation of mysticism, the first cause of mysticism is to create diversity. Put differently, diversity is the effect of the causal action of awareness.

In the mystical tradition, the relationship between cause and effect is the definition of karma. Simply put, karma is the carryover of an effect from a previous action. To the ancient mystics, all behaviors are the result of karma, whether we are talking about the carryover from a previous lifetime, the carryover of childhood patterns in our adult life, or the effects of an immediate action.

Awareness and karma are interrelated, since the more awareness we have, the more we can effect the future by eliminating behaviors that lead to negative outcomes. There are many forms of karma, but for the purpose of this book I focus on personal, family, and relationship karma.

The law of polarity—both the subject and the object: As soon as the singular source develops an awareness of itself, it becomes both a subject and an object, thus establishing the law of polarity. The law of polarity is the major identifiable force within the mystical structure of unity. By splitting the whole into representative parts, the law of polarity promotes diversity, without destroying the qualities of the whole in the process. Polarities constitute unity by bringing the whole into all subsequent parts and by giving all the parts a connection to the whole.

The biological process of mitosis is an everyday example of how we get a diverse population from a singular source. The zygote, the first cell of conception, contains the genetic history of the male sperm and female egg that united on its behalf. It contains the polarities of male and female within a singular framework. Through the splitting process of mitosis, the zygote transmits an exact image of itself to every successive cell in the developing embryo. The whole is now safely encased within every cell through the replication of its DNA, thereby connecting all cells within the organism to each other. This example illustrates how the whole is contained in the part and how the part is representative of the whole. The law of polarity operates on every level of existence so the integrity of the whole can be preserved in each individual part.

The Six Principles of Mysticism

At this point, we can establish the following six principles of mysticism in sequential order.

1. Unity is a characteristic common to all mystical systems.
2. Contemplation is the sense of awareness that unity has of itself.
3. By focusing on itself, unity transforms into dualities, establishing the law of polarity.
4. The resulting part and whole are the polarities defining mysticism and all other levels of reality.
5. The expansion of existence into other realities always contains the initial unity in its makeup.
6. The whole organizes the part, which contains the whole in its structure.

The concluding principle of mysticism, the whole is contained in the part, led Plato to conclude that we are born with the innate knowledge of the universe hidden within us. In the twentieth century, this concept was popularized by Jung's exploration into archetypal motifs. This part to whole philosophy allows us to see how ordinary occurrences in our lives contain the most extraordinary correspondences to the mystical.

In summary: the universe is a unity of its parts, just as the human body is a unity of its parts—they act differently and independently, yet perform as a single unit. Whether we are talking about mysticism, the human cell, or the human organism, the process of individual identity and collective functioning applies to every level of existence until we reach Ultimate Reality, where unity exists. Although we are separate people, we are also one people.

While we cannot speak of unity without destroying its presence, unity is nonetheless our spiritual parent, just as our mother and father are our physical parents. Perhaps the most remarkable thing about being human is that with two birthrights, we do not have to transcend our physical existence in order to find God. All we have to do is look within.

Establishing a True Self Through Mysticism

Our lives change when we encounter the mystical. But without a system to understand its principles, our intellectual capacity to learn from our exceptional experiences is reduced and we miss opportunities to grow. As the *Talmud* says, "teaching without a system makes learning difficult." In understanding the system presented in this book, we can see how even the smallest act of creation can be viewed in the context of much larger universal principles.

The goal is to develop a mature identity by establishing a true self; a responsive identity designed to transcend the natural patterns and restrictions so we can move into our future with greater intention and freedom. As we contemplate the vast number of possibilities available in a lifetime, we must ask: Why, in a life replete with choices and opportunities, do we insist on evoking the same reality over and over? Why do we continue to struggle? Why do we consistently attract the same types of relationships? Why is it so difficult to experience prolonged periods where we have peace of mind?

Creating a true self elevates the level of our choices. We are not simply repeating old patterns without knowing why, but are creating more conscious and responsible choices. We get what we want by being involved in our lives, rather than by reacting to what life has to offer. Instead of moving from one situation to another, we create a conscious life proactively, not restricted by unconscious fears and expectations. By moving past our ingrained constraints, we transcend our personal limitations and become greater. Here transcendence means the human drive toward expansion resulting from integrating the various parts of life into a conscious and coherent whole.

When we apply the study of mysticism to everyday life, personal growth happens. We move from smaller to larger contexts until we reach a level of wholeness where we feel complete within ourselves. To achieve this higher level of personality development, we have to overcome our limitations. In other words, we have to learn how to deal with the effects of previous situations on present life conditions. We will work toward this goal in subsequent chapters.

Summary

Mysticism refers to entering into the mystery of life and finding a deeper connection with the underlying forces of everyday experiences. Dating back to 500 B.C., mysticism is a philosophy of a singular source of life connecting everything to everything else. Although we are denied direct access to the singular source, we can see transformations of it all around us. Basic concepts presented in this chapter include:

- Mysticism is the understanding of how everything connects to everything else.
- Awareness occurs when the singular source focuses on itself, thereby bringing awareness of itself as both subject and object.
- Karma is the effect of an initial cause.
- Transcendence is going beyond constraint into a larger context.
- The central paradox is that we are simultaneously subject and object, individual and collective, separate and connected.
- The law of polarity, an emanation of the central paradox of mysticism, connects the mystical and physical levels to each other, while also connecting human experience to the mystical principles.
- Working through karma means transcending personal constraints, whether we are searching for enlightenment or just trying to get through the day.
- To understand the whole we must understand its parts.
- The universe is a unity of its parts, just as the human body is a unity of its parts, and they all act differently, yet they are still a unity.

The goal is to learn how to use ancient principles to transcend personal constraints and evolve into the true self. By integrating the mystical with the mundane, we experience a greater sense of empowerment and intention about how to live. When we begin to see the extraordinary in the ordinary, the enormous depth in simplicity, and how the entire universe manifests itself in even the smallest act of intention, we are drawn into a deeper reverence for life. Then each of us is able to find our own Angel from the Woods whenever we need her.

Chapter Two: The Law of Polarity

> *We have as One in us that which is living and dead, waking and sleeping, young and old: because these having transformed are those and those having transformed are these.*
>
> Heraclitus

W e live in a world of contradictions. Opposing forces pull us apart, sometimes dividing us against ourselves. But through their reconciliation, polarities offer a glimpse of the larger picture.

The 563BC Hindu legend of Siddhartha Gautama, relates how Buddha's reconciliation of polarities led to enlightenment. Born into a rich family, Siddhartha gave up his luxurious life and worldly attachments, including his wife and son, to find the true nature of reality. He adopted a wandering lifestyle dedicated to meditation. After years of homelessness and self-denial, he still had not found enlightenment. Fearing he would starve to death before he reached nirvana, he took a meal from a stranger. Thus, he began to forge a middle road between his former abundant life and his current ascetic existence. Soon after, he found enlightenment.

Like the Buddha, we must learn to integrate the polarities defining our lives to achieve balance and harmony.

Polarity in the Physical World

Polarities are everywhere, producing a flow of energy between two opposing points at many different levels. On a subatomic level, the attraction between the positive charge of the atom and the negative charge of the electron is the basis for the formation of molecules that give rise to liquid, gas, matter and life. On a biological level, male and female genders allow us to propagate our species. On a planetary level, the North and South Pole give the earth an axis to revolve around. On a physical level, magnetic poles produce electricity that runs generators and motors. In cosmology, black holes and white holes symbolize birth and rebirth on a cosmic scale.

The law of polarity operates on multiple levels simultaneously determining biological growth, energy transference, planetary, and galaxial stability. Just as carbon is an element found in stars, trees, trucks, and the human body, the law of polarity runs vertically throughout all levels of the universal hierarchy. Each level is determined by the flow between polarities and is related to the next because it is a functional part of a larger whole.

The Pulitzer Prize winning author, Douglas Hofstadter (1979), brings to light the relationship of the part to the whole. He explains that all "emergent" phenomena are actually "an interaction between levels. The top level reaches back down towards the bottom level and influences it, while at the same time being itself determined by the bottom level" (p. 709). According to Hofstadter, in an interrelated universe, everything on one level not only influences other levels, but also is a function of the whole.

The law of polarity addresses the interplay between polar positions, contrary points of view, and adjacent poles. It's the basis of life, thought, human development, and transcendence.

Any discussion of opposites must include the awareness that everything we observe, encounter, and experience is part of a larger whole. The following examples of prominent polarities demonstrate how wholeness is derived from its parts.

Observer versus observed: The observer cannot be separated from the observed, says Werner Heisenberg's (1962) uncertainty principle. By studying the direction and the momentum of subatomic particles, he discovered that whenever light was directed toward the particle being observed, the particle interacted with the light source producing a faulty reading. What was transmitted back to the observer was the direction or momentum of the particle relative to the light beam measuring it—not as the particle appeared in the natural world. Consequently, scientists studying subatomic particles have to deal in probabilities and not facts because they can never be sure what they are studying.

Through Heisenberg's scientific pursuits, the Western world accepts that reality exists in the context of the mutual interaction between the observer and the observed. Heisenberg showed we are connected as a unity. We are not just independently making judgments and measurements without the results reflecting our own intentions.

This insight was echoed by medieval Christian mystic Meister Eckhart who said, "The eye with which I see God is the very eye with which God sees me." As the central paradox of mysticism teaches us, the whole is the ground for all opposites. Once the whole perceives itself, it brings into existence the polarities of the seer and the seen, also known as the subject and the object.

As part of the whole, we have to take ourselves into account to gain knowledge about the object of our inquiry. When we look at ourselves, we see the reflection of the universe and when we study the universe we encounter ourselves again and again.

Particles versus waves: During the quantum revolution in physics, Niels Bohr (1958) introduced the idea that light has a dual personality. Under certain conditions light exhibits particle-like qualities and under other conditions it exhibits wave-like qualities. Just as particles and waves are inseparable characteristics of light, individuality and connection are inseparable human characteristics. Sometimes we act through individual need (particle) and sometimes we feel connected to something much greater than ourselves (wave). The diversity of the parts creates the unity of the whole.

Consistent with the central paradox of mysticism, Bohr used the word *complementarity* to represent the idea that the whole was divided into two opposing but complementing parts. He summed up his belief in one remarkable statement, "A great truth is a statement whose opposite is also a great truth." The particle-wave duality demonstrates that opposing truths and different realities are inseparable aspects of wholeness. Without one polarity to produce its opposite effect, we cannot comprehend the entirety of any experience as we have nothing to judge it against.

Causality versus noncausality: Since everything is connected to everything else, there are no disconnected or singular events in the universe, only those that are part of a larger interconnected network of impulses. Therefore, events never occur in isolation. They always emerge from a ubiquitous, but mostly unseen, level of existence.

There is an underlying context for every event occurring on the surface of reality. For example, a man may decide to move to another city for a better job opportunity. But there may be a deeper context outside of his awareness. He may be compelled by unseen convergent factors, such as timing, age, and the chance to meet a woman who would be a perfect match for him. Four months after the move to his new job, he shares a desk with his future wife.

Was this a coincidence? Not in the world of interconnected actions and experiences. Was he destined to meet his wife at his new job? Not necessarily. He could have chosen not to move, an action that would have collapsed all the possible realities in that context, but evoked other realities elsewhere. In a world of interconnections, we decide the path and the universe decides the realities that path will evoke.

Fate versus freedom: Any discussion about causality and noncausality brings up the question of fate versus freedom. Do we really have the freedom to choose, or is our fate predetermined?

Freedom is synonymous with free will, an attribute we can use to create our future. Fate is synonymous with determinism. Freedom gives choice in life; the body's fate, however, is determined by its finite existence. Fate belongs to the limited world of the planet, while freedom belongs to the infinite expanse of the spirit. Thus, fate is mortality played out against the background of infinite possibilities. Paradoxically, we have unlimited choice within a limited set of possibilities.

Since we are the embodiment of both freedom and fate, we must mediate between both realms so they become integrated within us. We need to respect the limits of what is possible while exploring our infinite potential. Each of us is responsible for connecting the polarities of freedom and fate in our lives. Each of us is a bridge, or a mediator, between these two extremes. In the context of fate, the laws of the planet bind us. In the context of freedom, our accomplishments are only limited by our imagination. Looking at freedom and fate as a unity, every action we take changes our fate.

Locality versus nonlocality: In the world of interconnection, events closest in space and time resonate with us more than distant events. In this sense, connection and memory go hand in hand. We remember events yesterday better than similar events a year ago.

But what about events of karmic consequences from past lives? These are called *nonlocal events*. Nonlocal events exist outside of the realm of our physical space and time (the lifetime of our body) and remain outside the range of memory.

In a world where everything effects everything else, events from a nonlocal time will effect our present day life. They are part of the web of interaction connecting us back through time. This mystical notion of unity is similar to the genetic connection we have to our ancestors. Through connection there is unity, through individuality there is diversity, and both are necessary for continuity and wholeness.

Mystics typically have access to nonlocal events, those far-off factors influencing our present lives. But we often fail to see the practical applications of nonlocal cause-and-effect thinking in the limited sensory perception world. Consequently, we relegate the mystic's recall to a realm not related to everyday events.

Karmic influences are always present. Since the whole organizes the part, we can find local and nonlocal influences present within us at all times.

Dependence versus independence: Through concepts such as separation and individuation, the self, the ego, and identity, Freudians and post Freudians have stressed independence as a sign of health. Consequently, words such as *dependency, fusion, co-dependency, isolation,* and *enmeshment* connote unhealthy associations.

In Japan, the word *amae* refers to the healthy Japanese need for dependency. Any blunting of this need creates a pathological condition the Japanese call *hinikuereta,* or warping (Doi, 1973). It is not surprising that Americans have the highest divorce rate, while 95% of Japanese children live in intact homes.

In the Western world, we are taught to be separate and stand on our own two feet. If you live with your parents as an adult, you are considered to be dependent in the pejorative sense of the word. In the Eastern world, dependency is a sign of respect and connection. Both positions are polarities defining the range between separation and connection. Rather than find a midpoint between dependency and independence, we tend to use our cultural norms as the standard of health.

This egocentric view of the world excludes other contexts that may provide reasonable balance. A rigid adherence to our cultural belief system destroys the ego's capacity for integration and synthesis on a larger scale. We may need to consider incremental moves from independence to interdependence. Japan's experience should serve as a healthy reminder that we may be too rigid in our adherence to the standard of independence.

Life versus death: Although the intermingling of life and death is natural, we have to train ourselves to view death as more than an end point. It is a sacred event, generating a vital force that gives meaning to life. This reciprocity connects the old to the young as the generations enter and depart in concert. It connects the physical reality of life to the metaphysical aspects of the spirit world. "Death is also the moment of a gift that the old give to the young, a last opportunity to teach about life," says Mary Catherine Bateson (1984), "but it is so shaped by accident and happenstance that the moment may pass and wisdom is often unexpressed" (p. 259).

Life and death are the most mysterious and mystical experiences we encounter. As with all polarities, life and death are intricately connected, coexisting on a grand scale in the same way any beginning seeks its completion through an ending. Our deaths are fixed with our first breaths. No sooner do we realize how good it is to be alive than we are faced with the fact that we are terminal. It is as if the universe determined start and end points for our lives and left it to us to define the *space in-between.*

Polarities in Everyday Life

The space in-between: At a time in our history when the struggle between *good* and *evil* is paramount, the question of what we do with the space in-between is even more urgent. Second only to the question, *Who am I?* the issue of how to deal with the poles of birth and death is worthy of complete dedication. Yet we seem to overlook it for more immediate, but less significant concerns. The value of life is put into proper perspective and given the critical sense of immediacy when juxtaposed to death.

To heal the universal splits in our everyday lives, we must first become aware of their existence. Awareness, as the first emanation of mysticism, is a powerful intervention. By becoming aware of how the world is divided and how it's replicated in physical reality, we can move off polar positions and find balance by exploring the space in-between.

In the *Nicomachean Ethics*, Aristotle defines the midpoint between two extremes as the *golden mean*. An example of the golden mean is found in the mythological tale of Icarus. King Minos holds Icarus and his father captive on an island. To escape, his father makes wings from wax, feathers, and string. He cautions Icarus to stay the middle course and not fly too close to the sun or water. In his exuberance, Icarus soars to the heavens until the warmth of the sun melts his wings and he falls to his death. The loss of balance cost Icarus his life. This myth shows how, having identified the extremes, we can maintain balance by finding the midpoint between excess and deficiency.

In a world where everything has an opposite pole, we are challenged to see both sides of every issue. We need to look beneath the surface for hidden contexts that expand the depth of our ordinary actions. Although individual actions have their own existence, they are part of an underlying organization of interactions. They do not stand solely on their own merits. The dynamic interactions of opposing tensions bring the world as we know it into existence. Resolving polar disparities is difficult since we typically view only one pole at a time and call it reality.

How we resolve polar disparities determines the strength and flexibility of identity and marks an essential learning curve. As opposing forces vie for dominance, we struggle to develop balanced identities and lifestyles to maintain a steady state, no matter the circumstances. We recognize people who are out of balance: they work too much, carry too much intensity, are abusive and disgruntled, or are prone to excesses and never seem satisfied. We go through periods when our lives are out of balance and we are stretched beyond our fingertips to cope with new and unexpected situations. With a solid foundation, these periods of fluctuation are opportunities for personality development.

One of life's greatest contradictions is the natural tendency to temper closeness with distance. By regularly engaging and separating from each other, we are often confused into thinking one position has privilege over the other. How can we separate from our parents, yet hold onto them at the same time? How can we fall in love without losing ourselves to our lovers? How can we be strong without making someone else weak? How can we have different perceptions of the same event and both be correct? These are typical contradictions we encounter every day.

Throughout this book we will see how the simple thread of the law of polarity draws us together and pulls us apart, while moving us forward from the initial merger with parents, through marriage, and ultimately to transcendence.

Summary

Polarities are everywhere, producing energy between two opposing points at many different levels. According to the law of polarity, the universe is unified—divided into parts that define the whole. We are microcosms or fragmented parts of the larger whole. Without one polarity to produce its opposite effect, we cannot comprehend the entirety of any experience.

Important concepts associated with the law of polarity include the following:

- Once the whole perceives itself, it brings into existence the polarities of the seer and the seen, also known as the subject and the object.
- There are no disconnected or singular events in the universe; every event has an underlying context.
- Events closest in space and time resonate with us more than distant events.
- We decide the paths our lives will take and the universe provides the resulting realities.
- We embody both freedom and fate and must mediate between them to become integrated. Fate belongs to the limited world of the planet, while freedom belongs to the infinite expanse of the spirit.

- Since karmic influences are always present, we can find local and nonlocal influences present within us at all times. Nonlocal events exist outside of the realm of physical space and time (the lifetime of our bodies) and remain outside the range of memory.
- In the Western world, we are taught to be separate and stand on our own. The success of Eastern cultures in maintaining nuclear families, signals that we may be too rigid in our adherence to the standard of independence.
- The tendency to temper closeness with distance is one of the great contradictions of life.
- Life and death are the most mysterious and mystical experiences we encounter. As if the universe determines start and end points, we are left to define the space in-between.

The dualities in our universe affirm the part to whole philosophy and show the importance of both poles in comprehending either. Whether we examine the soul, the psyche, the cosmos, or the atom, we are mystically teased by the endless polarities at all levels of reality.

Chapter Three: The Structure of Unity

All things are in process and nothing stays still, and comparing all things to flowing waters, we cannot step twice into the same river.

Heraclitus

The law of polarity governs micro and macro phenomena and provides a structural consistency connecting one level to the next. Since every level of interaction is part of a greater whole, we must understand the part to whole relationship to appreciate the law of polarity's comprehensive nature. Without the whole, we cannot define the part and without the part, we cannot comprehend the whole.

Emerson (1979) captures the essence of the part to whole association in this simple prose: "I am God in nature, I am a weed by the wall." Emerson shows us God is within nature and nature is within God. While a weed may appear to be insignificant compared to the great significance imbued in God, both are related. Without one we cannot define the other. If we did not know what was insignificant, we would never be able to understand the significance of God.

Ancient Structures Underlying Unity

During Heraclitus' lifetime in Greece, circa 440 BC, the world was seen as orderly and absolute; material things were solid, predictable, and unchanging. In Greek mythology, Chaos was the initial void giving birth to light, air, and earth. Out of the disorder of Chaos came the order of the natural world.

In contrast to the prevailing spirit of his time, Heraclitus saw the order of the universe existing through *opposing tensions*, producing a world in a constant state of flux and transition. In his view, order and disorder were connected, both being necessary to understand the unity of the universe.

To capture the essence of the underlying unity within a changeable world, Heraclitus formulated his now famous paradox of a river that can never be entered twice. Since river water is always moving, you may enter the same river at the same location, but you will be standing in different water. In fragment 22 he says, "All things are in process and nothing stays still, and comparing all things to flowing waters, we cannot step twice in the same river." In other words, although the river is in a constant state of flux, there is an underlying uniformity since the river's structure does not change. The river is still a river, although the water is constantly flowing downstream.

The analogy Heraclitus makes between life and change emphasizes that although things may appear familiar, nothing ever stays the same. We deal with a changing world all the time, yet there is an underlying organization to the change. Even though life events may appear to be disconnected, they hang together in a consistent way.

Two millennia later, in what would have appeared to Heraclitus like an act of sorcery, Isaac Newton co-founded a new branch of mathematics called calculus. He calculated and measured the rate of change and flow as one complete system.

Without the use of mathematical formulas, Heraclitus correctly reasoned that if the world was in a state of flux and transition, then all aspects of the world, including human beings, must be in the same state of flux. By relating the polarities of the macrocosm of the universe, with the microcosm of those who inhabit it, Heraclitus concluded there was a reciprocal and natural connection between the two, resulting in a unity of opposites.

In 1687, Newton again confirms the philosophy of Heraclitus by proving the connection among opposites in his third law of motion: *to any action there is always an opposite and equal reaction.* For example, as the wheels of a car spin backward the car is propelled forward, or as we step from a small boat onto the dock our forward motion pushes the boat backward. Whenever we have an action in one direction there is an equal reaction in the opposite direction. Action-reaction sequences always come in pairs.

The concept of opposing tensions in the Chinese culture preceded Heraclitus by more than 2500 years and Newton by almost 4500 years. The ancient symbol of yin and yang represents the polarities of male and female energy.

The Chinese oracle, *I Ching*, relied on the interaction of yin energy and yang energy for guidance. The interplay of these opposing energies provides the basis for the Chinese practice of acupuncture. Using the science of acupuncture (the placement and manipulation of small puncture wounds made by needles), physicians attempt to balance the body's energy systems by releasing male or female energy.

In each of the preceding examples, the law of polarity creates balance and harmony, as a change in one direction produces a corresponding change in the opposite direction ensuring the integrity of the entire system. Regulation of these opposing tensions determines the state of health. Many lives are out of balance because *the space between the poles is always overlooked for the sake of the poles themselves.*

A good illustration of this point is the current trend of urban professionals who leave well-paying jobs and move to remote areas to simplify their lives, only to return after a few short years, suffering from small-town burnout. Their logic lacks the awareness of a balance between the poles of urban complexity and rural simplicity.

We have a neurotic tendency to switch from one polar extreme to the other, thinking the opposite of what we are doing is needed. But the opposite is just more of the same from a different direction. It is like being stuck between the extremes of eating uncontrollably and crash dieting while wondering why the weight will not stay off. Without balance, the results are the same no matter which pole we take to solve the problem. Balance, the relative state of equilibrium between opposing forces, can only come from a keen understanding of the role polarities play in achieving it.

An outcast living in the hills above Ephesus, Heraclitus lived in a time of reciprocation between people and the heavens not seen today. According to the ancient *law of correspondence*, there was a complementary synchronization between the energy of the earth and the energy of the heavens, connecting the halves to each other.

Since there were no artificial light sources, the heavens were as much a part of everyday life as reading by artificial light is today. Great mythological figures, representing seen and unseen natural forces, affected the Greek culture and belief system. Mythology today is nothing more than a good story—a metaphor so far removed from our daily lives, its cultural meaning has become irrelevant to the Western world.

Additionally, our circadian rhythms no longer correspond to the sunrise, sunset, and shifts in the night sky as they did 2500 years ago.

Daylight Saving Time throws them off even more. Consequently, we have lost our place within the universal time clock. Towns no longer organize around City Hall or the clock tower. Everyone carries the clock tower on his wrist.

Community has given way to individuality. Astrology and fixed stars have been relegated to the uncorroborated science of metaphysics. Today the Western world is ruled by modern science and predicated on *proof* and *facts*, not on the immutable relationship between people, nature, and the heavens. Yet our connection to the larger whole remains vital. What was once an accepted way of life—being part of the structure of the universe—we term *cosmology*.

Heraclitus saw things differently, viewing the relationship between people and the universe as having a bi-directional flow. The universe was the macro structure and the people who participated in it were the micro structure, making each structure necessary for the existence of the whole. As each polarity gave definition and meaning to the other, a system of connection and correspondences among all system components was created.

Modern Structures Underlying Unity

In our modern world, we have lost touch with the other half of our existence. We have taken the mystery out of life by severing our connection to the cosmos. We now see it as something to conquer, explore, and understand rather than as an estranged part of ourselves.

But some researchers have gone beyond our contemporary model of how ideas relate to each other to find correspondences on cultural, biological, and scientific levels that connect us to the world at large. These progressive paradigms keep us from becoming entirely alienated from our mystical heritage and remind us of the correspondences we have to larger structures of existence.

Jung and synchronicity: Synchronicity implies wholeness—the connection to an underlying pattern that unites each of us with the events and people in our lives. Jung (1959) coined the word *synchronicity* to describe this deep fundamental connection we share.

In a synchronistic world, the timing of every event is intricately connected to a larger web of interactions beyond human awareness.

There are no coincidences. Although individual actions have their own existence, they are part of an underlying organization of interactions. They do not stand on their own merits.

Through this interrelated system of interactions, people and events are systematically connected to each other. One event is complete within itself and part of a larger structure of events. Similarly, one cell is complete within itself and part of a larger constellation of cells.

Jung's most notable example of synchronicity came from his work with a patient who was emotionally inaccessible to him. For anything to develop in the therapy, there had to be an unexpected and illogical event to burst her intellectual defensiveness. One day as Jung sat with her in therapy, she reported a dream where someone had given her a piece of jewelry, a golden scarab. As she related the dream, Jung heard a scratching on the window. When he opened the window, a large insect flew into the room. He caught it in his hand and discovered it was a scarab beetle with an iridescent color, like a golden scarab. Jung handed the insect to his client saying, "Here is your scarab." Because of this synchronistic event, the therapeutic impasse was broken and the patient became more accessible to treatment.

Levi-Strauss and structuralism: The connection between human enterprise and cultural determination is the basis for the structuralism of French anthropologist Levi-Strauss (1963). He studied the causal connection between the internal structure of tribal members' private belief systems and the external myths of the tribe. Levi-Strauss called this relationship *deep structure* because the structural organization of the tribe's internal and external world was homologous.

Structuralism is the study of wholeness, since no part can be considered independently from its relationship to other parts of the system. Put differently, people cannot be considered apart from their environmental contexts. The point for Levi-Strauss is not that people and cultures are reciprocal, but that people and cultures are interconnected.

Carolyn Myss (1996) analyzed the interconnected structural pattern between people and their cultures during the1930s polio epidemic. The crippling of America was both internal and external. Those most susceptible to the crippling disease were already economically crippled from the depression. "American children," explained Myss, "were as susceptible to the viral disease as to the economic dis-ease. This sense of being crippled was so quickly woven into the tribal psyche that American voters even elected a president crippled by the polio virus" (p. 106). According to Myss, the same pattern was embedded in the psyche of the American culture across subsystem boundaries. At the end of World War II, when America felt a collective sense of being whole again, the environmental context was stable enough to support the discovery of Salk's polio vaccine. As the cultural context changed, so did the polio epidemic, leaving Americans feeling more hopeful about the future. In this example, Myss tied the economic, political, physical, and psychological levels of the American culture to the common thread of helplessness and hopefulness.

Von Bertalanffy and General System Theory: Just as structuralism is the study of an underlying unity connecting people and culture, von Bertalanffy's (1968) General System Theory connects principles governing different living systems to each other.

By showing the correspondences between one system to another, von Bertalanffy eliminated duplicative principles in different fields of enquiry. His General System Theory views the relations connecting the part to the whole. It merges the sciences by elevating systems to a unity of their parts rather than reducing systems to the parts themselves.

As a biologist, von Bertalanffy believed living systems contain patterns of relationships to protect or restore wholeness. Many of his concepts, such as homeostasis, equifinality, and perspectivism have been adopted by family therapists.

Von Bertalanffy focused on how different levels of existence are governed by the same underlying structure. With the sensibilities of a mystic, he perceived that systems, divergently different in size and scope, operate under the same principles. For von Bertalanffy, General System Theory was a unifying force bringing together different fields of study under one consistent rule. It became a science of wholeness rather than a system of principles governing how people behave.

Bateson and the ecological perspective: The ecological view is closely identified with Gregory Bateson, a social scientist and anthropologist, who thought it was absurd to try to split mind from matter. Bateson devoted his life to finding patterns connecting one species to another and all species to the larger ecosystem. He was quoted as looking for a pattern connecting "the crab to the lobster and the orchid to the primrose and all four of them to me. And me to you" (1979, p. 8). Like his contemporaries Jung, Levi-Strauss, and von Bertalanffy, Bateson believed the world contained common links and focused on how human systems were part of the total ecological balance of the planet. He theorized we live in a world where events and ideas interact, producing reciprocal relationships between mind and nature.

For his work on the double-bind theory of schizophrenia, Bateson is deemed a founding father of "systems family therapy." In his landmark paper on schizophrenia (Bateson, Jackson, Haley, & Weakland, 1956), he demonstrated how psychotic breakdowns logically follow family messages containing inconsistent or double meanings. The patient is unable to discriminate between one meaning and another. The breakdown occurs when the patient's frustration level rises to an intolerable point within a family system that offers no relief. Bateson's early schizophrenia work shows wholeness as a unifying factor, by examining the effects of family variables on individual functioning. His position deviated from the prevailing 1950s psychoanalytic emphasis on individual performance.

Like von Bertalanffy, whose ideas were applied to family therapy, Bateson was not a psychotherapist. He was a social scientist searching for the common link among all things. Yet, he became revered in a field he did not pursue. The translation of the ideas from one field of study to another, underscores how different levels of life are governed by the same underlying structure.

Chaos Theory: In science, the paradox of unity and disparity has been rejuvenated by Chaos Theory, the study of self-similar structures embedded in nonlinear, or chaotic, systems (Gleick, 1987). In analyzing these systems, scientists found they have remarkable structures and predictable internal organizations, even though they appear to be disorderly. For example, water coming out of a faucet at a certain rate of speed looks uniform and appears to have a consistent flow. As the rate of the water is reduced, the flow becomes uneven and the water appears to sputter. Under closer examination, the uneven flow has a consistent underlying pattern. What appears to be discontinuous on one level is actually consistent on another level. Thus, synchronicity, structuralism, General System Theory, ecology, and Chaos Theory show the underlying uniformity existing among different levels of reality.

The growing trend towards uniformity, in the light of chaos or random occurrences, signals the interdependence among all things and all actions. In an interconnected universe, causal and acausal events, as well as personal and impersonal experiences, are part of an underlying and unifying pattern. Eminent astrophysicist Arthur Eddington (1923) emphasized "Space is not a lot of points close together; it is a lot of distances interlocked." Looking from ancient Heraclitus to these modern views of wholeness and connection, we can see the uniformity of thinking throughout the centuries.

Summary

This chapter explored the underlying structure of unity by drawing parallels between the macro and micro levels. From the atom to the universe and from the cell to the living organism, the law of polarity is fixed, absolute, and unchangeable. Its universal nature means that it can be found at all levels of existence, from the beginning of the universe to the beginning of the fetus.

We examined the conformity between modern thought and ancient philosophy to gain a historical basis for the law of polarity. Major concepts include:

- Heraclitus taught his students that the world is in a continual state of flux as energy oscillates between polar positions; yet within the constant fluctuation of energy there is an underlying reciprocation between the macrocosm and the microcosm that connects everything to everything else.
- The basis of the ancient Chinese practice of acupuncture is to bring the body into health by balancing the polarities of male (yin) and female (yang) energy.
- For Jung, correspondences exist within the psyche of people, a collective psyche of shared experiences.
- The structuralism of Levi-Strauss connects people to their cultures, and the myths of different cultures to each other through the underlying uniformity of their cultural structures.

- Von Bertalanffy connects processes that govern different entities to each other through the uniformity of the processes that regulate them.
- Bateson views nature and mind as forming one organism thereby creating an entire ecological web of interaction through patterns that connect everything to everything else.

In subsequent chapters, we will see how the law of polarity is embedded in the human experience, from birth to transcendence, with a uniformity and regularity that makes even the most mundane experiences close cousins to the otherworldliness of mysticism.

Chapter Four: Presuppositions of Identity Formation

I searched my nature.
Heraclitus

Heraclitus explained how all events are related through the underlying connection between opposites. Health and disease define each other, as do good and evil. This is a simple, yet deep concept. As we try to change bad habits, we can attest that simple never means easy.

This chapter focuses on identity formation within the context of polarities. The ideas build an integral framework for personality expansion as discussed in subsequent chapters.

The Complexity of Simplicity

Humans have a tendency to complicate issues rather than simplify them. This trait inspired the English philosopher William of Ockham to proclaim that explanations should be kept as simple as possible. His principle, known as *Ockham's Razor*, illustrates how we complicate problems beyond necessity, often obscuring the real issues. While it appears simple to identify the ingredients of a good life, it is difficult to combine them into the exact mixture desired. This leaves many of us obsessing over our shortcomings.

The following example from my practice typifies the pattern. Jim was raised by cold and distant parents who were never satisfied with his accomplishments. Consequently, he grew up feeling he was not good enough and developed behaviors to protect himself from criticism. The result was extreme social isolation, leading him to call me for help. Since rejection was at the core of his behavior, his associations to rejection had to change for his behavior to change.

Changing a behavior is not easy to do. It's like pulling one continuous thread in a fabric and watching it snag and distort the pattern as it comes free. Similar to threads in a woven cloth, our behaviors are interconnected with our personalities. Changing any behavior precipitates a change in the entire internal makeup.

Although the reason for Jim's isolation was obvious, I could not say, "Look Jim, you must get back out into the world now that you know why you're living in isolation." It was not that easy.

Simple, yet deep—the Pythagorean Theorem: We can see a different perspective in the work of the Greek mathematician, Pythagoras. He was a well-known mystic of his time and founder of the Pythagorean movement. According to him, math was the language of the universe and held the key to understanding the earth and its place in the cosmos.

The Pythagorean Theorem is more than just a form of geometry. It sets the standard for formal proof creating the scientific foundation for mathematics. The theorem, $x^2 + y^2 = z^2$ says that the sum of the squares of any two sides of a right triangle is equal to the square of the hypotenuse. The Pythagorean Theorem is true for any right triangle imaginable to infinity. In other words, it is always true, there is no subjectivity involved, and it can never be disproved.

We can begin to see how a simple theorem is deceptively deep. But this is just the tip of its depth. "Pythagoras theorem provides us with an equation that is true of all right-angled triangles" says physicist Simon Singh (1997). "And that therefore also defines the right angle itself. In turn, the right angle defines the perpendicular and the perpendicular defines the dimensions—length, width, and height—of the space in which we live. Ultimately, mathematics, via the right-angled triangle, defines the very structure of our three-dimensional world" (p. 18). The simplicity and depth of the Pythagorean Theory contains a truth so profound, it reverberates throughout space and time and into infinity.

A profound and deep understanding of a subject is met by an unsuspecting sense of beauty and simplicity. Beauty, simplicity, and depth are mystical qualities Pythagoras brought to light in stunning fashion. These powerful concepts can be found in ordinary life. A meaningful coincidence, the innocent truth blurted by a child, the beautiful pose of a single rose, and the rapture of a sudden insight carry these mystical characteristics.

In self-consumption, we find ourselves searching for life's deeper complexities, only to miss the simple truths before us. It is just too obvious to see them.

Once we understand that the simple things are the deepest, we can pay attention to the obvious issues in our lives. Because it is easier to identify the cause of a problem, we dwell in hours of self-discovery rather than act upon a problem. We surmise going deeper will make the necessary action come easier, but it does not. So we keep searching. Although it is simple to catalogue a box of photos or to clean out a closet, why do we refrain from doing these things? We avoid the simple things because they are the gateway to deeper patterns within us.

I tell my clients that the first goal of therapy is to produce enough awareness for a conscious understanding of the problem. Although it can be trying for my clients, I can help uncover the behavioral and emotional sequences underlying their current patterns.

The second aspect of therapy is frustrating for therapist and client alike—doing something about the problem. Both facets of therapy are equally important, but during the second part we discover that *simple equals deep, not easy.*

The Paradox of Action

Building on the notion that simple equals deep, not easy, we often encounter a distressing paradox. Although we know how to make our lives better, it seems difficult to act upon that knowledge. Rather than act, we rationalize, intellectualize, and repress. We have developed so many unique defense mechanisms, psychotherapists are always studying new psychological abstractions and continually reinventing the field.

While struggling with every conceivable solution except the one that works, we avoid taking reasonable risks to enhance our lives. Why is it so hard to take a simple action? I have searched my consciousness, and those of my clients, for years to understand why we make life so difficult. I can only conclude we do so because it is how we learn. In other words, making things difficult is an important and necessary part of living. Logically, if making life difficult were not necessary, we would not do it.

The polarity of *simplicity* is *complexity* and we tend to make things more complex than they really are. If there were a simpler way, we would take it. But we often do not. Why? My answer: because simple equals deep, not easy.

It is easier for us to do what is familiar, even if the results are negative, than to do something different. In fact, the worse things get, the harder we work at what is not working, thinking the extra effort will make the difference. The only difference it makes is to frustrate us even more. Ironically, we tend to do whatever possible to make life harder and then try harder still to make it easier. Caught in this redundant loop we feel there is no way out and become constrained.

The Power of Constraints

The cycle of hard work begetting more hard work cramps our style. It's like ill-fitting clothes pinching in the inseam and tugging under the arms, preventing spontaneous and free movement. Every movement produces a constraint. We try to move beyond by doing what is familiar, but only know how to make clothes of the same dimensions, so the cycle begins again. Sometimes we change the clothing material or style, hoping for a better fit, but still experience the pinches and tugs.

The habitual use of the same template for each new situation produces repetitive patterns causing us to yearn for freedom. We become so fed up with our limitations, we throw caution to the wind and try something completely new. Only after we suffer and have nothing more to lose, do we take the blind leap of faith into the future. Miraculously, we land on our feet.

Edward O. Wilson (1998), one of the foremost scientists of our time, looked at what motivates people and concluded the tension between the problem and the solution drives learning forward. Whether we are figuring out the solution to a mathematical equation or playing out an internal dialogue, we are trying to solve something. What to eat for dinner. What to wear to work. How to get more money to pay the bills or to take a vacation. What to do today and tomorrow. Since tension influences the creative process, only the rare individual can create for the sake of creating.

There is a fundamental redundancy to our behavior. We compulsively relearn what we already know because we become habituated to the struggle and forget there is a simpler way. Freud's (1920) notion of a repetition compulsion, a continuous although pathological attempt to *get it right*, characterizes this redundant loop.

We fool ourselves into thinking we are making progress when we undo negative situations created by our persistent actions. For example, take the vast number of people who are proud to be clean and sober when abstinence only returns them to where they were before they started drinking. The same is true of former smokers and drug users who rejoice in their restraint from indulging after years of struggling with their addictions. These people, with their whole lives ahead of them, end up working hard just to stay alive. It is a wonder we make any progress at all, given the need to complicate our lives. But, we do learn from our mistakes; therefore making mistakes is a sign of hope.

The paradox at the heart of the learning lesson is: negative loops provide the fuel for positive growth. This is what Heraclitus meant in fragment 18 when he wrote, "It is necessary to know that conflict is universal and that strife is right, and that all things happen through strife and necessity." In other words, the tension between the problem and the solution is a learning opportunity.

"Everything that happens, including humiliations, embarrassments, misfortunes, all has been given like clay," Borges (1999), the foremost Argentinean author wrote, "Like material for one's art ...Those things are given to us to transform, so that we may make from the miserable circumstances of our lives things that are eternal, or aspire to be so." Borges, who slowly lost his sight until he was legally blind in his old age, explained, "If a blind man thinks this way, he is saved. Blindness, is a gift" (p.483). It is the unusual person, such as Borges, who can see a constraint as a gift.

The Significance of Anxiety

Most constraints produce anxiety because of the irrational fear of the unknown. These fears are not reserved for negative anticipation. We can fear success as much as failure.

Anxiety also is associated with the fear of known things, such as traumas we try to repress. Freud (1900) believed we repress content too overwhelming for the ego. Once the content is repressed, we can go about our day-to-day lives until the repressed material returns to consciousness and infuses us with anxiety.

Thus, Freud thought anxiety was the failure of repression to do its job. He (1926) later shifted his view, believing anxiety was the central dynamic causing repression. Anxiety resided under the mechanism of repression and was the cause of it. Freud's shift in thinking guided many therapists from attempting to uncover repressed material to teaching people to manage anxiety so repression was not necessary.

Long before Freud, Kierkegaard (1844) argued that anxiety arises each time we confront the possibility of moving beyond the constraint. Kierkegaard saw anxiety coupled to freedom. The greater the potential freedom, the more anxious we become.

For Kierkegaard, constraints represent limitations and anxiety represents the potential necessary to move beyond the constraint. That is, anxiety occurs at the point between constraint and breakthrough. Any movement beyond a constraint is considered a forward movement, a step up the hierarchy. If successfully negotiated, it results in a stronger and more adaptable personality structure.

May (1950) theorized the number of steps we can take with anxiety as the teacher is endless, since it propels us to the next rung on the ladder. If we turn our back on anxiety-producing things, we never learn anything new and stop growing.

This is where Freud's repression theory enters the philosophical picture. If anxiety causes repression, then it is a natural process to repress any anxiety-producing stimulus and act like it is not there. Out of sight out of mind, so to speak. Consequently, if we do not know we are not growing, then who is to say we are not growing? We are more comfortable locked in the vault of constraints than living in the threatening world of possibilities. Repression of anxiety gives us control, but comes at the exacting price of forward movement.

Self-reflection and Language

There will always be some anxiety in our lives, producing repetitive patterns and habituated behaviors. As self-reflective people, we can determine the source of anxiety and know how to alleviate it. Once we develop sufficient insight based on our reflective abilities, we can change our behaviors to support the outcomes we desire.

To understand anxiety, we must view it in relationship to self-reflection. How do we know we are anxious? Our bodies tell us with quickened pulses and sweaty palms. Our minds alert us with redundant thoughts of fretful outcomes. But, to realize we are anxious, we must identify anxiety as anxiety. In other words, we must become aware of it.

Our abilities to label our feelings, contemplate their sources, and determine how to change them, are specific to human beings. In the animal world, when a cat lunges at a mouse and does not catch it, the cat does not berate itself. It waits for another mouse to come along. Cats do not have low self-esteem. They do not tell themselves stories about how they need to be quicker, wittier, or more congenial. They work on instinct. Although cats have certain advantages in their heightened senses allowing them a better chance to survive in the wild, they do not form concepts, build bridges, or read books. They do not store vast amounts of general knowledge in their heads for retrieval. Cats build an instinctive history based on survival, not an intellectual history based on concepts.

Alfred Korzybski (1933), in *Science and Sanity*, contended that the animal mind is bound to its particular space because it relies on the senses to ensure its survival. The human mind relies on language to develop concepts, allowing us to pass information to others through time. This eliminates the need to discover the same things over and over again. Ultimately, language distinguishes human life from animal life and permits self-reflection to play a dominant role.

When Heraclitus said, "I searched my nature," in fragment 53, he was affirming the basic human trait of personal exploration and inner reflection. This is where anxiety and self-reflection merge. We are aware not only of infinite possibilities, but of our constraints in light of those possibilities.

Becker (1973) writes stirringly about our conflicts as we create realities out of visions while lower animal forms fight daily for physical survival. "The fall into self-consciousness, the emergence from comfortable ignorance in nature, had one great penalty for man: it gave him *dread*, or anxiety" (p.69). As self-reflective beings, we are aware of our potential, our constraints, and ourselves.

Self-reflection is only possible through the use of language. Although we have access to both the physical and mystical worlds, we have only one vehicle for communicating our experiences, language. We analyze, explain, and classify everything according to words.

Some philosophers, called *radical constructivists*, believe reality is dependent on language. Since thought is dependent on language, without language we could not think and without thinking we could not discern reality. Therefore, reality cannot exist independent from thought, which is dependent on language.

On the other hand, Platonists argue there are two realities, one seen and subjected to language and the other unseen and pure, beyond language. In either case, language is a significant characteristic associated with humans.

The trap of language: The physical body can only generate feelings, but self-reflection allows for labeling those feelings. The ability to self-reflect accounts for feelings of guilt, shame, joy, and satisfaction. The body does not distinguish between joy and sadness, but it signals feeling states we define in one way or another.

In a Wittgensteinian sense, we are *trapped in language*, perpetuated in the mental health field by relying heavily on labels to characterize deficits. With therapists becoming more sophisticated in behavioral psychology, vocabulary resulting from deficit-model thinking is expanding at an alarming rate. "This language is slowly disseminated to the public at large," said social psychologist Kenneth Gergen (1991), "so that they too can become conscious of mental health issues. As people acquire the vocabulary, they also come to see self and other in these terms" (p. 15). It seems the more diagnostic codes we have, the more pathology we find.

We face the paradox of language: without it we cannot communicate effectively and with it we miscommunicate by generalizing reality and calling it fact. Since language is imprecise, we can only communicate a close approximation of how we feel. However, feelings are not facts and do not necessarily correlate with a specific situation. For example, I may feel hurt when my spouse does not pay me enough attention because it activates an old childhood pattern of neglect. Yet my spouse may be preoccupied with her own thoughts and not responding to me at all. From my childhood neglect, I associate a lack of attention with being hurt and act accordingly. I feel hurt, but my feeling is not a fact. My wife did not hurt me. We build our belief systems and reactions from these kinds of generalizations.

The use of language was considered a mechanism of distortion by Lao-tzu and the ancient mystics. In his linguistic model, Korzybski agreed that the ability to generalize results in the misevaluation of nonverbal as well as verbal cues. Two of Korzybski's famous quotes are, "The map is not the territory" and "The word is not the thing." The perception of reality is not reality itself. By demonstrating the difference between a *word* and a *thing*, Korzybski addresses the penchant for treating feelings as if they are facts or real things, when in reality they are not.

We create levels of abstraction between our initial feelings and how we label them and the labels are often wrong. We talk to ourselves using words to support the patterns we have perpetuated since childhood. Over time the story line, language, and pattern become one seamless part of personal identity.

In the attempt to become bigger and to step outside the restrictions of our ancestors, we are constrained by language. As Lynne Twist (2003) said in exposing the myth of scarcity, "We can't always change the circumstances that surround us, but we can choose the conversation we generate about them" (p. 219). To move beyond our constraints we must change the language we use.

Healing polarities through language: Since language is such a powerful force, we must take care not to perpetuate old patterns and belief systems through it. Awareness of how we mirror our beliefs through language can produce alternative realities. We can use language to support the outcomes we desire, rather than maintain established patterns. To overcome language restrictions, we need new ways of thinking such as: (1) using sentences to describe events rather than one-word labels; (2) using strengths to balance the conditioned use of deficit-model descriptors, and; (3) realizing how language correlates to our previous mental models and perpetuates their realities.

Summary

In this chapter, identity formation was explained within the context of polarities, anxiety, self-reflection, awareness, constraints, and language. We have a tendency to complicate problems and avoid the simple things, because they tap into deep patterns within us. It is easier for us to repeat familiar behaviors, even if the effects are negative, than to do something different. Caught in redundant loops, we feel constrained. The resulting anxiety can propel us to move beyond constraints to self-reflection and growth. Major concepts include:

- The simplest things are the deepest things.
- The essential paradox is to figure out why it is so difficult to take the actions to make our lives better.
- Anxiety signals a problem and occurs at the point between constraint and breakthrough.
- The task is to move beyond constraint to growth.
- Since everything is a learning opportunity, there are no mistakes.
- Awareness is a constituent of self-reflection and the means to understand and change behaviors.
- We need to be aware of how personal language can perpetuate behavioral patterns from childhood and restrict growth.
- To overcome language restrictions, we must change language patterns to eliminate labels that emphasize weaknesses.

Understanding these concepts, we can change the normal tendency toward learning hard lessons and resisting inevitable ones. We can act through conscious intention, rather than through habituated behavior patterns. As a result, we can have more conflict-free time to extend our lives in purposeful and meaningful directions.

Section Two: Personal Development and Mysticism

Chapter Five: From Merger to Differentiation

> *It is necessary to know that conflict is universal and that strife is right, and that all things happen through strife and necessity.*
>
> Heraclitus

Ideally, we would like to approach the future without being drawn into effects of the past. But the interplay of past patterns and future dreams provides the necessary tension for growth. This section focuses on how early childhood patterns extend to marital choices and pull us into old patterns. These behaviors constrain us until we learn to transcend them and move forward. Although steeped in psychology, this section is entirely based on the law of polarity.

Early Childhood Identification

Opposing tensions and identity formation: At every stage of existence as we drift in and out of relationships, we are challenged to identify who we are. As we develop, we connect and separate from our parents, our peer groups, our mates and eventually life itself. Throughout our lives, we experience continual movement between the polarities of connection and separation. If we fail to separate adequately from others, we become enmeshed with them and lose our boundaries and sense of ourselves. On the other hand, if we fail to connect with others, we become disengaged and end up isolated and alone. The poles of separation and connection, called freedom and commitment in adulthood, are embedded within every relationship. A significant part of life's work is to determine the balance between these two poles.

Since our early caregivers influence us, we develop our identities based on associations and reactions to them. Consequently, two poles arise from the interactions—we either identify with them, act like them, and emulate them (connection), or we counter-identify with them, and become reactionary by not acting like them (separation).

The reaction against parents results in a reactive personality, not a conscious one. When we say, "I don't want to be like that" we are trying *not* to become something, rather than being self-determining. On the other hand, when we identify with our parents and say we want to be just like them, we are constraining the future by developing their same limitations.

Even for those who were orphaned, raised by single parents, or adopted, the poles are significant. A client told me his father played no role in his life. He had never met him and did not have any feelings towards him. Since he never knew anything different than being raised by his mother and brothers, the absence of his father was not damaging or relevant. However, he was always going to *be there* for his son, no matter what. The transparency of this statement makes his father's importance in his life obvious.

Symbiosis: Like the tension between the oneness of mysticism and the diversity of experience, the polarities of connection and separation are an ingrained human experience.

Each of us is born out of the merger with our mother. In the womb, we experience the internal atmosphere she creates. After birth, we rely on her to create a safe external environment.

Newborn children merge into a symbiotic union with their mothers. The mutual bonds are so intense, should anything happen to either, the other would not be able to thrive. For mother and child alike, it is a time of incredible vulnerability, dependency, and joy.

The symbiotic state is seductive because the total immersion makes each feel as one person. The child has no self/object separation and therefore no self-consciousness, just a semiconscious dream state. The mother regresses in service to her child, creating a fusion often exclusive of others.

In the Buddhist tradition, the experience of the world without objects and divisions is called "nirvana." Symbiosis can be nirvana-like in its experience of the mystical quality of oneness.

As infants, we live in interior space, feeling our way around and having our needs satisfied to the extent of the physical and emotional availability of our mothers. The first six weeks of life are subjective because there is no sense of an external reality. At this stage, infants cannot make the distinction between their own tension-reducing activities and those of their mothers.

The immense comfort in the merger with the mother exists with the dread of dependency, causing anxiety. Because of that dread, at some distant level infants know they are capable of sacrificing independence to stave off anxiety. Kierkegaard associated this with moving into a new stage of life.

For a healthy transition from symbiosis to independence, infants must learn to balance the polarity of connection and separation so the loss of attachment does not overwhelm them with anxiety. We can only imagine the distress infants feel, crying in the middle of the night waiting for someone to soothe their needs and the relief they experience when those needs are pacified. No wonder they are reluctant to do anything to jeopardize the tension-relieving relationship.

To grow, we must separate from our mothers, but this task produces enormous ambivalence. If we separate too completely, we run the risk of losing the one person we are dependent on for well-being. If we don't separate, we never become independent and risk becoming hopelessly compliant.

At this early stage of development, the forces establishing the poles of separation and connection are set. To embark on the path of independence, each infant must leave the mystical union with his mother behind. While mysticism speaks of wholeness relative to the spiritual mother, the human task is to become a more complete and self-sufficient individual. This different kind of wholeness must be tempered with the right degree of physical dependence on the mother.

A central preoccupation of D. W. Winnicott (1951), an early pioneer in ego psychology, was the concept of a transitional object, such as a blanket or favorite toy. Children use transitional objects to soothe themselves during the process of separation. Prior to the introduction of a transitional object, the function of soothing the child is left primarily to the mother. In making the transition from being mother-focused to becoming self-focused, the child uses a transitional object to reduce the anxiety of separation. The transitional object facilitates a successful transition from merger to separation. It preserves the continuity of contact between parent and child, avoiding a breach as the child moves into an objective relationship with the environment. The transitional object reassures the child that being independent is possible, while giving the child an initial sense of self-reliance. The early stage of merger and differentiation produces anxiety that lingers as we struggle to balance the polarities of separation and connection.

Internalization: The process of identity formation begins as the child transitions from symbiosis to separation. According to Mahler (1975), another pioneering ego psychologist, symbiosis occurs during the second month of life. Prior to the symbiotic stage, the child lives in a relatively undifferentiated space and depends upon the mother for survival. For the child, it is a time when the *I* is not yet differentiated from the *not-I* and in which inside and outside are only gradually coming to be sensed as different" (p. 44). The lack of differentiation between I and not-I is the primary reason children refer to themselves as *me* when they become verbal. We hear children say, "Me go to the zoo," instead of "I am going to the zoo." This primary form of identification exists because infants see themselves first as objects to someone else before they see themselves as separate beings.

Once the consciousness of an independent I comes into awareness, the child becomes both a subject and an object. The child now knows he can soothe himself. He can make the distinction between an outside agent and an internal process. At this point, the child's relationships to the outside world become as important as his feelings about those relationships. In other words, the inside of the child and the outside of the child have equal significance.

According to object relational theory, the emergence of the interpersonal child occurs when he becomes aware of internal experiences satisfied externally. That is, the child monitors awareness of the external world as it relates to the satisfaction of his internal needs and expands or contracts his contact with his environment accordingly. To effectively deal with relationships, the child must not only negotiate the polarities of separation and connection, but also the polarities of his internal and external worlds.

As a result of symbiosis, the child unconsciously absorbs selective parental attitudes and points of view into his internal world. The process of absorption occurs before the development of a self-aware I and does not allow the child to discriminate between what is being absorbed and what is not. As a result, the child identifies with certain aspects of his parents at an unconscious level. Ego theorists call this process *internalization* and believe it provides the foundation for ego stability and further ego development. These representations become the basis for our present and future behavior patterns. They serve as models of behavior and remain constant, even as we mature.

Jung (1921) introduced the term *imago* to signify an internalized image containing the qualities and traits of important people in our lives, usually parents. Psychologists have also used terms such as *mirroring, incorporation, imitation, modeling,* and *assimilation* to describe this process of internalization. Becker (1962) sums up the process of identification through internalization by noting that:

> Identification takes place only *after* the child's attempt to carry through satisfying action is blocked by the parent...As the action is stopped he literally doubles up on himself, and can no longer continue the forward momentum of energy by completing an *external* act. The energy then must find its outlet in the process of *adapting to the parent*, and to his commands—and no longer in the child's own spontaneous act. This is how the child incorporates the image of the parent and the parent's displeasures, and makes them slavishly and uncritically his own (p. 59).

According to Becker, early identification is an unconscious process until the child is forced to identify himself by determining what he is not able to do. For the typical child, everything goes along smoothly until he is told *no*. This simple word limits his world and starts a process of restriction defining his early personality.

Parents decide where, when, and how often to use the word no. Parents who do not believe in saying no must determine how to communicate that the child has breached a barrier. Once told no, the role of the child is to make sure no means no. He pushes the limit until the parent establishes a firm barrier he respects. Then the child internalizes the restriction by doing something he should not do and saying no. For example, he may pull the nose on his mother's face while saying, no.

The word no defines two poles essential to personality development: *I am,* and its corresponding part *I can,* and the polar opposite, *I am not,* and its corresponding part *I can not.* These two poles form the basis for identity development. The law of polarity becomes more clearly defined as the self-aware I emerges after the early stages of differentiation. But in the early stages of personality development, the sense of I am, and I am not, become powerful identity statements for the child.

I am, I am not: It is only fitting that one of the most powerful statements in the history of humankind contains the words *I Am*. When Moses delivered the Ten Commandments to the Jews at Mount Sinai, he asked God, "Who shall I say sent me with these laws unto you?" To which God answered, "Tell them that I Am sent you."

In the Jewish religion, there are more than ninety different ways to say God. None of them can reach the true essence of The Eternal's spirit because once the name of God is put into the spoken language, the word limits its definition. The experience of God, the divine consciousness, has no name because God exists beyond language. Just as Lao-tzu pronounced *the name that can be named is not the eternal name*, it is impossible to capture holiness.

In the words of German theologian Rudolph Otto, God is *numinous*. It is a holy name because its meaning is ineffable. In some texts it is written as G – D, because to spell the word out completely gives a false impression of its meaning.

From the mystical story of Moses, comes the perennial concept of I am, the shortest sentence in the human language and the greatest identifier of the unique spirit within each human being. The task for each of us is to connect with our uniqueness, our true self, and to consciously identify ourselves. Thus, the question *Who am I?* is at the heart of the developmental quest.

Identifying who we are is fundamentally related to the process of separation. It begins with the first movement away from our parents as we struggle to roll over, then crawl, and finally walk on our own. As young children, we are elated as each developmental stage allows us to explore the world a little more independently. With our first steps come our first bumps and bruises, along with the reality that we never stop moving toward greater independence.

As we explore the world, we differentiate and separate from our parents, marking the end of symbiosis. The process of identification now begins. During the stage of separation and exploration, parents baby proof their homes from the unrelenting curiosity of their mobile toddlers.

Continuing to separate from our parents, we interact with them through a developing sense of being different from them. We no longer experience ourselves as being merged, but as being separate. We have increasing control over our bodies and know how to soothe ourselves. What our mothers once did for us, we can now do for ourselves to some extent.

Kohut (1971) refers to internalizations used to soothe and nurture ourselves as *transmuting internalizations*. These internalizations become part of us and are no longer viewed as separate or outside of ourselves. As the sense of self coheres, we select from the environment the actions and behaviors of our parents that make us feel good. We identify with them.

I call these early identifications *I am*, because they give us a better sense of what we like. I term those actions that make us feel bad, our counter-identifications, *I am not,* because they identify us through negation.

The act of identification through negation is found in those of the Ten Commandments beginning with the words *Thou shalt not*. By identifying what we should not do, we are establishing the polar position for what constitutes correct action. The same is true in personality development.

The identification of what we are *not* creates the identity of what we *are*, even if it is a negative identity. "We will cling to a negative self-identity," says Welwood (2000), "even if it is choking us, because it gives us a sense of existence—'I am something rather than nothing'" (p. 26). In other words, by negation we establish a point of identification for ourselves as much as we do through direct identification. The Greek word for affirmation by negation is *apophasis*, which literally means *alluding to something by denying it*. The Jewish scholar Adin Steinsaltz (1998) reminds us that this form of identification was originally called *grasping by rejection* by the ancient Sages. "For there is a comprehensive grasp through positive confirmation," says Steinsaltz, "and there is a comprehension through negation or reduction, by recognizing what it is not" (p.137).

Unfortunately, the natural process of identification through negation leaves us short of grasping our true selves. Ideally, each of us would use the nascent identification as a foundation for further exploration into a deeper and more conscious sense of self. Instead, we develop identities based on early reactions and attractions and they unconsciously form the bases of our developing personalities.

For Winnicott (1945), a *false self* develops when a child constantly reacts to impingements placed on him by his mother. The false self is not a conscious identity because it is based on either reacting to people (I am not) or by copying people (I am), and not on true beliefs or honest interactions. By being compliant, or oppositional, a child does not develop healthy coping skills. Rather he creates a system of defenses to deal with life's challenges. This false self becomes a coping style keeping the "true self" submerged until the false self so utterly fails, there is no harm in the true self coming out.

As children, we do not have the ability to consciously draw distinctions between what we like and dislike. By the time we are capable of such discrimination, our behavior patterns are set. At some point we may become so rigid in accepting or rejecting our parents, we become all or nothing, polarized in our attitudes towards them. When this happens, we find ourselves fighting intensely with them about insignificant things or we acquiesce and become compliant.

Differentiation and Identity Development

An interesting and largely unconscious process takes place as we separate from our parents. We use their same or opposite personality characteristics as the basis for choosing our peers and mates. This unconscious process explains why some people appeal to us and others do not. If we identify with our parents, we usually develop friendships with people they find desirable. If we counter-identify with our parents, we develop friendships with people who do not meet with their approval. It is uncanny how many parents pull out their hair over their children's choice of friends and mates. In an attempt to define ourselves as not being like our parents, we often bring home people who represent their opposite pole and, predictably, are the ones they find the most objectionable.

The process of identification gives the child an early sense of self and at the same time he becomes more self-aware. This dual process is responsible for the crisis of separation—by separating from the object of identification, the child incurs the threat of losing the object. The early awareness the child has of separation is commonly referred to as "separation anxiety." If the child fails to separate adequately, he risks sacrificing his independence for the sake of security. This will have negative consequences later in life when independence holds a higher value.

As we mature, the conflict between separation and connection gets played out again and again in our adult relationships. The dynamics of relationship development, relationship health, and relationship maintenance are constant focal points in our lives. How close should I get to other people? What is the risk? Will I lose myself in the relationship if I do not assert myself? Yet, if I assert myself, will I risk losing my partner? These adult dilemmas are evident in the early childhood process of separation.

Splitting and Personality Development

Analogous to the initial split of the singular source into a subject/object duality, a child splits from the symbiotic merger with his mother to develop his own sense of being in the world. As he separates, he encounters the first of many contradictions he will face in his life.

At every stage of our lives, we deal with the contradiction of being independent and self-determining human beings who are also emotionally dependent. The infant moves from merger to separation from mother; the adult deals with merger and separation in marriage; the elderly deal with separation from life. The balance between separation and merger is a constant reminder of our connection to the central paradox of mysticism—defining the universe as being both part (separate) and whole (connected) at the same time.

Movement from emotional dependency to emotional independence creates much anxiety in children and raises the question: How can children retain autonomy in the light of their overwhelming dependency needs?

Psychoanalyst Melanie Klein (1929), believed that children deal with this ambivalence by instinctively splitting the world into *good* and *bad* polarities. Through splitting, negative feelings toward the object of separation can be encapsulated and not interfere with the task of detachment.

It is normal for a child to feel both love and hatred towards his mother since she is a source of nurturing, as well as a source of frustration. But any negative feelings threaten the child's emotional security. Splitting becomes a way for the ego to maintain its integrity in the light of this overwhelming anxiety. To establish a relative balance between separation and connection, the child has to reconcile the idealized good parent with the demanding bad parent.

Rather than feeling the conflict of being divided by his own ambivalence, the child divides the world into good and bad parts. This early defense mechanism lays the foundation for understanding the adult conflict of attachment and autonomy in marriage.

Splitting in Marriage

The primitive defense mechanism of splitting is also present in marriage as newlyweds advance from the initial stage of marital bliss to being separate people who share a marital connection. The early stages of marriage produce what family therapist, Murray Bowen (1978), calls *fusion*; a mutual resonance between the partners so if one is happy, the other is happy and if one is sad, the other is sad. They have the ability to trigger reactions in each other as if the two separate people are actually one.

Since marriage is similar to the initial fusion of the parent-child relationship, we experience the earlier parent-child ambivalence of autonomy and attachment. During the normal developmental course of marriage, negative feelings occur between spouses, creating anxiety. As negativity increases, the good feelings associated with the earlier part of the marriage become overshadowed by anxiety from the negative feelings.

To deal with these negative feelings, spouses split the marriage into good and bad components. Then they project their unresolved childhood issues of autonomy and attachment onto each other. One spouse becomes good and the other bad.

They see each other through the distortion of their own projections, so the "bad" one is always the other person. "I am OK, my wife is not," the husband thinks, "because if she would only be more agreeable everything would be fine." This is the same kind of distortion accompanying common complaints about parents, bosses, jobs, children, and even former therapists. We think the problem is always *their* fault. We fail to realize that splitting involves the projection of unconscious feelings onto other people. The process turns our own dissatisfactions into a statement about someone else, leaving us to live in the past more than the present.

We cannot get away from ourselves easily because we attract whatever we disown. As the ancient Hindu saying goes, "That art thou," or in the words of Walt Kelly's most famous creation, Pogo, "We have met the enemy and he is us." In the end, the adult task is to understand that we split the world into polarities to protect ourselves against the anxiety of holding contradictory feelings. We need to learn how to integrate these contradictions rather than project them onto others.

Summary

The law of polarity is embedded in the beginning of personality development and sets the stage for future relationships. As we develop relationships throughout our lives, we are challenged to identify who we are. Major concepts include the following:

- Symbiosis, beginning in infancy when we merge with our mothers, is a representative human experience similar to the mystical quality of oneness.
- Because comfort in the dependency causes anxiety, infants must balance connection and separation to move toward independence.
- Children use objects to soothe themselves and handle separation anxiety.
- Infants must negotiate the polarities of separation and connection in addition to the polarities of their internal and external worlds.
- Following symbiosis, the child absorbs selective parental attitudes and these internalizations serve as models of behavior.

- The word *no* defines two poles essential to personality development: I am, and its corresponding part I can, and the polar opposite, I am not, and its corresponding part I can not.
- The identification of what we are not creates the identity of what we are, even if it is a negative identity.
- In splitting, a defense mechanism for dealing with ambivalence during separation, children divide the world into good and bad polarities.
- Splitting is present in marriage as newlyweds advance from the honeymoon bliss of oneness to separate people sharing a marital connection.

In adult relationships, the conflict between separation and connection continues. Early forms of identification stay into adulthood where they are challenged to become more flexible and adaptable as life conditions change. If we do not meet life's challenge with a certain degree of awareness, the self-protecting behavior becomes a limitation.

Since marriage is similar to the initial fusion of the parent-child relationship, it arouses earlier parent-child ambivalence of autonomy and attachment. In marriage, we may have distorted projections and view the other spouse as the "bad" one.

We need to learn to integrate these contradictions rather than project them onto others. If left unresolved, they will continue to haunt us. Since we cannot get away from ourselves, we will always attract what we disown.

Chapter Six: Family Patterns and Styles in Marriage

*Everything taken together is whole
but also not whole, what is being
brought together and taken apart,
what is in tune and out of tune; out
of diversity there comes unity, and
out of unity diversity.*

Heraclitus

Just as the sperm and the egg perpetuate likeness through an invisible blueprint generating another human being, the family contains a behavioral blueprint handed down through generations. It does not matter whether we identify or counter-identify with our parents, we still absorb their behavior patterns and reproduce them throughout our lives, thus preserving and transmitting them.

Sometimes this is hard to accept, especially if we do not like our parents' behaviors. In an attempt to disassociate from them, we may shift to opposite poles, actively denying we were influenced by them in the first place. It is impossible to tell an adolescent in open rebellion his parents are influencing him. He will only increase the intensity of his behavior to prove his accuser wrong. It is far more important for him to be his *own person* than to analyze the origins of his behavior. From this reactive position, the teen will predictably become the opposite, further strengthening his association to the object of his rebellion. Paradoxically, our attempts to become completely unlike our parents increase the intensity of our connection to them.

Family Patterns

By identifying patterns and associating them with our parents and their parents, we see the links to our ancestors on many different levels. This linkage gives the concepts of internalization and identification a mystical hue.

Family karma: The handing down of effects from one generation to the next, becomes more than just a metaphysical construct when viewed as the transmission of patterns through many generations. Bowen (1978) coined the term *intergenerational transmission* to describe the historical behavioral links passed from one generation to the next. These intergenerational transmissions connect family members to each other karmically. All members carry the same family limitations, even if they act in contrary ways.

A classic example of intergenerational transmission comes from Amy Tan's (1989) acclaimed novel *The Joy Luck Club,* in which she chronicles three generations of relationships among Chinese women. She shows how four Chinese mothers could not keep their own cultural patterns from influencing their children's lives no matter how hard they tried. The book is an intricate weaving of twelve stories connecting four Chinese immigrants with their American-born daughters. Their dialogues are filled with tension contrasting the repressive Chinese regime the mothers endured and the relative ease of life experienced by their American daughters. In each story, the mother uses strength and resourcefulness to redeem herself from a bad marriage suffered in China. Coming from a nonsupportive culture, these mothers switched to the opposite pole in raising their children. They wanted their daughters strong and to be treated as equals in marriage. But as their daughters married, the mothers realized the patterns they shunned, such as passiveness and unassertiveness, were inherited by their children anyway. As An-mei, the mother of Ruth, said of her Chinese upbringing, "I was raised the Chinese way: I was taught to desire nothing, to swallow other peoples' misery, and to eat my own bitterness. And even though I taught my daughter the opposite, still she came out the same way!" (p. 215).

These stories, brilliantly told by Tan, are examples of how we bring patterns from previous generations into our lives, even though we consciously try not to visit them upon our children. An-mei acknowledges the karmic connection with her mother and her daughter by reasoning, "All of us are like stairs, one step after another, going up and down, but all going the same way." The stairs in An-mei's metaphor link the generations, before and after, to each other in restriction and opportunity. Tan shows how the intergenerational patterns of repression, submissiveness, and self-sacrifice are also complemented by patterns of cunning, strength, and perseverance inherited by Ruth and the other daughters to break the karmic repressive pattern. As with An-mei and

Ruth, within the prison of our ancestral patterns, we can find the keys to freedom.

The Joy Luck Club provides vivid examples of family karma and its effect on subsequent generations. The following case examples further illustrate how the back and forth movement, from one pole to another, preserves family patterns in subsequent generations.

Case Examples

Case one—Keeping the pain alive: Robert, who was neglected as a child, tacitly vowed never to neglect his children when he became a father. Consequently, as a father he became smothering, overbearing, and altogether too involved. He was *not his parents* to an extreme. By counter-identifying with his parents, he never made conscious decisions about how he would act, just conscious decisions about how he would not act. This identity through negation created what Winnicott calls a false self. Robert related strongly to the fact that he was neglected as a child and never took his behavior to any other discernable level than its opposite manifestation.

Robert came to therapy because his son was acting out. Early in the assessment it was apparent there was not enough space for his son to be independent—he could not even have his own thoughts without his father's intrusion. Robert was so attentive as a parent, his child began pushing him away just to have some breathing room. After awhile this dynamic turned into a power struggle. The more his son pushed him away, the more Robert pursued him, vowing to never neglect him like he was neglected. By the time Robert came to see me, the situation was out of control. Although his approach to parenting was the exact opposite of his father's, the pattern was the same. Robert became as neglectful of his child's needs as his father was of his needs.

Robert's struggle not to inflict his childhood pain on his child shows concretely how we keep our parents alive within us, even as we try to undo their inevitable influence. By moving to the opposite pole, Robert created the same reaction in his child he had experienced towards his parents. It was an unfortunate outcome, but one he could have avoided if he understood the law of polarity. Although Robert's style was different from his father's—he did the opposite of what was done to him—it produced the same pattern. His vow not to be like his father, guaranteed the same result. Robert did not make a change that made a difference, but did the opposite of what was done to him.

Case two—*Jealousy:* We carry indelible impressions of our parents from the cradle to the grave. These impressions exert a tremendous force, whether we are conscious of them or not, whether we accept them or not, and whether we like them or not.

In his autobiography, Nobel Prize-winning author Elias Canetti (1999) carves patterns out of ordinary life experiences, painstakingly showing how everyday events contain the seeds of future behavior patterns. His insights are keen and perceptive as he explores the forces shaping human development and personality. In one instance, he writes how, as a young boy, his father's sudden death was "pushed into" him by his mother's loud, mournful cries. Her reaction was so profound, Canetti could not dissociate his mother's painful experience from his own reaction. His father's death was forced into him by his mother's intensity. While his mother mourned externally, Canetti did the opposite; he internalized his hurt feelings and kept them to himself. From that moment on, he was her fierce protector and became insanely jealous whenever a suitor came her way. "At this point," Canetti admits, "the jealousy that tortured me all my life commenced." By protecting his mother, Canetti was able to physically do something about the grief of losing his father. But there was a price to pay, a lesson to learn. The pattern of his jealousy was his constant reminder of an interior wound that would not heal. In his adult relationships, he became extremely jealous whenever there was a threat of loss, real or imagined, because of his association of pain to the sudden loss of his father.

Case three—*Anger:* Monty Roberts (1996) provides another example of polarity patterns in his book, *The Man Who Listens to Horses*. As a child, Monty was humiliated and beaten by his father, a sergeant with the local police force. After seeing his father brutalize a suspected thief, Monty vowed never to be like him. He moved to the opposite pole and completely divorced himself from his father's behavior. Having developed a genuine sensitivity and patience with horses, he created a humanitarian training method devoid of spirit-breaking practices. Monty's choice was simple—either become a brute like his father or go to the opposite pole and develop a sensitive, life-affirming nature.

Adding to the complexity of human behavior, we often repress the parental aspects we want to disown. When we shift to the opposite pole, we do not disown the negativity of the developmental environment, we deny it. In other words, we do not remember it exists. We become *unlike* it, so it becomes *uncommon* to us. In Monty's case, he repressed the anger towards his father. If he chose to recognize the anger, it would have made him just as explosive as his father. As a result of this counter-identification, Monty had to consciously control his instinct towards rage. As he became aware of this dynamic, he developed a more conscious identity.

Relationship Styles

Each of us has internalized patterns constraining our natural expressions. Just as Canetti had to resolve the pattern of his jealous nature, and An-mei's daughter had to resolve her pattern of submissiveness, and Monty had to resolve his pattern of anger, we must identify and resolve our repetitive patterns.

Bateson (1972) has identified three common types of marital relationships—*complementary*, *symmetrical*, and *reciprocal*—where long-standing patterns seek resolution. The complementary and symmetrical relationships are based on polar entrenchments imbued in similarities and differences between marital partners. The reciprocal relationship is the most balanced of the three.

When people who are complementary or symmetrical meet, they respond like tuning forks, vibrating in exact agreement. The resonance results in deep-souled and unmistakable feelings we call love. Unfortunately, we do not realize these feelings come from shared unconscious identifications and counter-identifications. Underneath the surface, we are resonating to primitive internalizations corresponding to our own levels of constraint, or as Bowen says, to similar levels of differentiation. Since internalizations are static and do not change as we mature, we may remain unaware of such hidden levels of attraction for years until we find ourselves struggling with adult entanglements remarkably similar to our childhood patterns.

Complementary relationships: In complementary relationships, partners have opposing, but complementary styles, such as dominance/submission. Partners cling to opposite poles, reinforcing the complementary balance needed to sustain such relationships, since they are based on accepted differences in power.

Each partner adheres to one pole while relying upon the other person to provide the balance through the opposite position. Problems arise when the pair entrenches in rigid opposition. Rather than taking advantage of the other person's attributes, each partner reacts to the other's difference with increasing intensity until the relationship becomes entrenched. Then neither partner gives in, instead adhering to his or her position, causing the relationship to stagnate.

Kate and John exemplify the complementary relationship. When they married John was controlling and definitive in his views. Kate was much quieter and did not have strong opinions. They engaged in hours of conversation as Kate listened to John talk about his future plans. Kate was supportive and added a few points John found interesting. As their relationship matured, John's strong views turned to doctrines and Kate's support waned and she began to withdraw. Viewing Kate's withdrawal as rejection, John became stronger in his demands. By the fifth year of their marriage, Kate and John were polarized. What was once a complementary exchange of love and support turned into a polarized relationship characterized by aggression and withdrawal. Attempting to regain their former balance, John insisted that Kate be more assertive and Kate insisted that John be more sensitive.

Kate and John illustrate how opposite poles are initially attracted to each other while setting the stage for future entrenchment. By engaging the opposite pole, each has access to a wider range of possibilities, fueling the attraction. But over time, each partner tries to mold the other in his or her own image. The insistence upon sameness within a complementary relationship threatens the balance. It puts pressure on one partner to give in, thus producing the oppositional quality characteristic of entrenched relationships. As a result, the initial attractors slowly degenerate and become detractors.

Symmetrical relationships: In symmetrical relationships, two people have similar behaviors, but neither gives in when conflict arises.

Both partners have the need to be right, even when they are saying the same thing. Symmetrical relationships are based on equal power.

In symmetrical relationships, partners have the same representational patterns and are attracted because they share similar interests. The eventual entrenchment results from the lack of divergence in the relationship. Every relationship needs a flow between two poles to create the essential tension that keeps relationships vital. In symmetrical relationships, the tension is created through competition. Symmetrical partners fight about everything.

In the following example, Sam and Carol are in general agreement with each other, but spend their energy disagreeing about a minor point. They hire a babysitter to have an evening out and agree she should not make too many personal phone calls while babysitting. Carol feels the teen should not be expected to spend all night without having contact with her friends. Sam feels Carol is being unreasonable since the babysitter should devote full attention to her paid job, even if his children are sleeping. Sam and Carol fight over this issue, even though they agree some phone calls are okay as long as the sitter does not spend too much time on the phone. Sam is not saying the sitter should not be on the phone and Carol is not saying she should have carte blanche. But they act as if the other is expressing those ideas. Once they understand they agree on the basic issue, they begin to fight about what constitutes "too many" phone calls. The more they fight, the more they fall into a typical communicative loop: Sam says he is controlling to balance Carol's leniency and Carol says she is lenient to compensate for Sam's rigidity. Breaking down the communication into a simple pattern we see Carol is actually as rigid as Sam because she adheres strictly to her assertion that Sam is rigid. In other words, they are both rigid and fighting about who is at fault. This is what I call *projective blame* because the blaming person is guilty of the same faulty behavior. The loop continues as Carol projects her rigidity onto Sam, while assuming a more lenient position. Sam then justifies his rigidity by citing Carol's leniency in his defense.

Redundant loops: The communication loops created through complementary or symmetrical relationship styles are called *self-referential*. The assertion each partner makes says as much about the sender of the message as it does about the intended receiver. For example, John's insistence that Kate be more assertive says as much about his assertive style as it does about her submissiveness.

Also, the communication is *recursive* because the couple tends to come back to the same loop and the argument begins all over again. The most common example of a self-referential statement is the *liar's paradox* whose origin goes back to the ancient Crete's of Greece. This paradox is focused on the Cretan who proclaims, "All Cretans lie." As Keeney (1983) points out "If he is lying, he tells the truth. If he is telling the truth, he lies" (p. 29). The recursive loop created by the Cretan who lies by telling the truth, and tells the truth by lying, intensifies the more you focus on it. The interpreter ends up at the beginning of the loop without any resolution to the statement. The law of polarity is at work within Cretan's recursive statement as the reader moves back and forth between the poles of truth and falsity without any resolution.

Sam and Carol's pattern is a good illustration of a redundant loop. Sam asserts he is being rigid because Carol is being lenient and Carol asserts she is lenient because Sam is so strict. As Carol and Sam perpetuate this loop, they create what Wachtel (1993) calls *vicious circles*. Since neither partner is willing to break the loop by giving in or changing behavior, each continues to oppose the other.

Bateson (1972) refers to this never-ending loop of stubborn opposition as *schismogenesis*. Each partner is married to his or her position more than to the other person, a condition that causes the relationship to stagnate. In *complementary schismogenesis*, the couple becomes increasingly more distant, while in *symmetrical schismogenesis* there is an increase in rivalry. In either case, the couple deflects energy away from creating *we-ness* and eliminates any possibility of achieving a higher level of functioning in the relationship.

Redundant loops are very difficult to break, especially when they become entrenched. In subsequent chapters, I will show how to break these loops by using interventions consistent with the law of polarity.

Reciprocal relationships: In reciprocal relationships there is an easy balance, a give and take allowing each partner to move from one pole to the other. Since there is no entrenchment and no desire to change the other person, the relationship is healthy and flexible. Partners feel an increasing sense of satisfaction because they have access to each other.

In fact, when reciprocal relationships are under marital stress they do not reciprocate negativity. They maintain their overall balance by allowing for negativity without responding in kind. Consequently, themes of dominance, submission, hostility, and resentment play out in relatively fast cycles without having a chance to become habituated.

Further, reciprocal relationships reflect an appreciation of the wholeness provided. The relationship is larger than either individual and together the partners can attain what is not possible separately. This is considered a respectful middle position compared to the polar entrenchments of complementary relationships and the competition found in symmetrical relationships.

Summary

This chapter focused on family karma, the behavioral blueprint handed down through generations, and its affect on interpersonal relationships. When we are aware of our inherited patterns, we can learn to act consciously and break generational loops.

In one case study, a man vowed not to inflict his childhood pain of neglect on his child and moved to the opposite pole of behavior. By suffocating his child, he created the same reaction he had experienced towards his parents and his son pushed him away. In another case study, a man's jealousy was traced to a childhood incident—the sudden loss of his father. A third case study illustrated how counter-identification with a brutal father resulted in gentle, life-affirming behavior with animals.

Analyzing how long-standing patterns seek resolution in relationships, Bateson identified three common types of marital relationships—complementary, symmetrical, and reciprocal. Basic concepts include the following:

- Complementary relationships are based on opposite polar entrenchments. When partners insist on sameness, the balance of the relationship is threatened. Partners are pressured to give into each other, thus producing the oppositional quality characteristic of entrenched relationships.
- In symmetrical relationships, partners are attracted because they share similar patterns. Since the lack of divergence in the

relationship results in a lack of tension, the partners create conflict through competition.

- The communication loops in complementary or symmetrical relationship styles are termed self-referential because the blaming partner exhibits the same faulty behaviors.
- The communication is called recursive because the partners perpetuate the same loops thereby repeating the same arguments. Until one partner gives in or changes behavior, the oppositional communication, termed schismogenesis, continues.
- In complementary schismogenesis, the couple becomes more distant, while in symmetrical schismogenesis rivalry increases.
- In reciprocal relationships, an easy balance allows partners to move from one pole to the other, resulting in healthy and flexible interactions. The relationship is larger than either individual, allowing the couple to attain what is not possible separately.

When we understand our inherited patterns and their effects on our relationships, we can find the keys to freedom.

Chapter Seven: The Law of Polarity and Marriage

Nature prefers to hide.
Heraclitus

From conception to death, we are in relationships with others. In adulthood, the most basic and significant relationship is with a partner, often in a marriage. But marriage is not an easy relationship to maintain, as indicated by the 50 percent failure rate of first marriages and 60 percent failure rate of second marriages. These staggering statistics reflect the *disposal society* characteristic of our culture. I am not suggesting couples stay together at all costs; sometimes it is more important to walk away from a bad situation. But the 50 percent failure rate reflects the difficulties associated with sustaining significant relationships.

In adult arenas, such as marriage, we can grow beyond the restrictions of childhood experiences to deal with their karmic effects. Marriage is the relationship that challenges us to resolve our personal patterns, repair the dualities of our earlier identifications and counter-identifications, and connect with our true selves. Failure to do so, results in multiple relationships with people who reset the same karmic structure. To resolve our patterns, we must have them set again. Thus, we are compelled to choose mates who will reset the patterns needing resolution. In that way, we can become more complete.

Polarities and Patterns in Relationships

The attraction force: People are drawn to each other based on an underlying effect, or resonance, between them. I (1993) previously referred to this magnetism as the *attraction force*. Freud identified this concept as *unconscious perception* and Zukov (1989) termed it *the law of attraction.*

The attraction force brings us into contact with people who excite us, both positively and negatively, and who force us to delve into ourselves to resolve deep-seated behavior patterns. We are drawn to each other based on the early childhood styles and parental patterns internalized as *imagos*.

Using Bateson's relationship terminology, when two similar imagos resonate, a symmetrical match creates feelings of familiarity and recognition, commonly called love. When two dissimilar imagos resonate, a complementary match provides a sense of completion, also called love. In attracting the same or opposite imagos, we extend unresolved childhood issues into adulthood and recreate family patterns in marriage.

As we attempt to resolve unfinished circumstances through the attraction of like and opposite imagos we are drawn deeper into the marriage. In the process we project the expectations of our imagos onto our mate. The influence of our mental models is so strong, we select the actions, statements, and attitudes befitting our preconceived notions, relegating other interactions to a lesser role. By struggling against our own projections we unconsciously try to work out our unresolved childhood issues.

By being selective, we get what we expect because our expectations lead to fulfillment. According to Watzlawick (1984), the basis of the self-fulfilling prophecy "is an assumption or prediction that, purely as a result of having been made, causes the expected or predicted event to occur and thus confirms its own accuracy" (p. 95). Originally identified by psychologist Thomas Merton (1949), it was also known as the *Pygmalion Effect*, after George Bernard Shaw's play where the Pygmalion character falls so hopelessly in love with a female sculpture, it comes to life. Likewise, the belief in future events can be so strong as to be superimposed on current events until the prophecy comes true.

Debbie is a good example of how this process works. Her father was a loud, demanding, and intimidating man who Debbie feared. Although he never struck her, Debbie felt abused. Her father also had a soft side and was quite fond of her, but his threatening demeanor overshadowed his love. As Debbie got older, her imago of him led her to believe that any man or authority figure who was loud and demanding was also abusive, even if he was trying to be helpful. As time went on, Debbie's imago of her father became an expectation transferred onto similar situations. Her husband was loud, demanding, and fond of her, but she felt abused by him.

Sometimes it takes several bad relationships to get the picture. In Debbie's case, she married a man similar to her father and then shifted to the opposite pole when she had a child. She raised her son with excessive care not to be abusive. As a result of her *polar shift*, she overindulged him, cramping his space and causing him to lash out at her. He became the predictable imago of her father—abusive. Now Debbie had to deal with abuse from all sides, her father, husband, and child.

Similar to Robert's case in the previous chapter, this situation was created through polar shifting, where Debbie attracted one pole in marriage and acted out the opposite pole in raising her son. Either way, the results were the same: Debbie felt abused. As an adult, Debbie had fulfilled her expectation for how she was going to be treated, ignoring any evidence to the contrary.

The attraction force is characterized by the uncanny ability to attract those who either reflect our belief structures or are diametrically opposed to them. Those we attract are not the same as our parents, but carry similar patterns. Ultimately, we are forced to define ourselves more fully as we live through continual reenactments of childhood themes.

To answer the fundamental question as to why human beings learn through repetition, we can refer to this supposition: repetitive loops provide the fuel for positive growth. We are problem solvers who require growth experiences and if we do not have an equation to solve, we lose our opportunity to grow. Repetitive behavior patterns provide the fuel for growth and remain until they are resolved.

Polar shifting: We shift to the opposite pole in our attempts to resolve our fears and anxieties resulting from our previous attachments. Freud (1965) saw this shift as a defensive reaction against the harmful effects of negative desires or environments and termed it *reaction formation*. For example, if I feel rage toward my father, I may determine rage is a dangerous emotion. If I act on it, my father may rage back at me, causing greater fear and anxiety, not to mention physical harm. To protect against his reaction to my rage, I decide to become overly sweet and engaging. In this polar shift I limit the potential danger of my own aggressive impulses by shifting them to the opposite pole of compliance. This is a natural shift because aggression and compliance are two extremes along the same continuum. In other words, both traits exist at the same time, one overt and one covert. Instead of incorporating a potentially damaging trait, we turn the other cheek. Thus, we reduce the fear of being damaged by our own aggressive tendencies.

The shift to the opposite pole reinforces the fact that the world is split into good and bad possibilities. In an idiosyncratic manner, we determine which elements to keep and which to project.

The process of moving from one extreme to the other in our love relationships is illustrated in Thomas Mann's (1993) first novel, *The Buddenbrooks*. Set in eighteenth century Germany, the novel depicts the decline of an influential bourgeois family over the course of four generations. The Buddenbrook family history begins and ends with Antoinette (Toni) Buddenbrook. At the beginning, she is introduced as the eight-year-old granddaughter of Johann Buddenbrook, founder of the family business. The reader is treated to marriages, births, deaths, divorces, and the political pressures of maintaining German bourgeois status. At the end, some forty-two years later, Toni is one of the few surviving family members.

Toni's pattern of multiple marriages shows the effects of the law of polarity. Her first husband was cunning with surface respectability and ambition, but underneath, he was greedy and dishonest. His drive to power led to his downfall. The marriage was doomed from the start because Toni married for the outward appearances, motivated by the Buddenbrook legacy to remain among the upper class of the German bourgeois. Over time, she realized social position did not make up for a lack of kindness and commitment and could not reconcile these two positions. In her second marriage, she chose a man with opposite traits. He was kind and attentive, but had no desire for social status, no drive to the top; he was comfortable just "muddling through." Although she tried to stay married to this decent man, she missed her connection with her family's power and notoriety. Her first husband was elegant but "black internally," while her second husband was easy going, but had no drive. Because she could not resolve these opposites within herself, both marriages were doomed to fail.

The opposite is still the same: Have you ever had the experience of meeting someone you really care about, only to end up feeling you must have been hallucinating? In moments of despair you ask, *What was I thinking?* Exhausted and wounded by such relationships, you vow never to experience the pain again. Instead, you go for the opposite, someone with no resemblance whatsoever to your former lover.

This is a common dilemma, a rather normal process with a simple root traceable to Heraclitus. In fragment twenty Heraclitus says, "Good and bad are the same." We are attracted to one pole or the other, to its likeness and its opposite.

The world is composed of opposing tensions. The traits we think attracted us often become the characteristics we resist—their opposites. Some of us have a never-ending stream of negative relationships, causing our family and friends to wonder if we will ever learn. When we finally shed the maladaptive relationships, we opt for their opposites. We will not make the same mistakes twice! Until we become conscious of how polarity effects our lives, these opposing forces will determine our options and leave little chance to experience the space in between.

Shifting between opposite poles, we miss the big picture containing patterns requiring alterations. Thus, we bounce around looking for the right person only to fall into despair at the futility of it all.

Bateson showed how two people could have opposing views of the same situation, as if they were in two separate relationships. Termed *monocular vision*, this one-sidedness is analogous to a person viewing the world through one eye. It takes the perspective of both partners to get the full picture of the whole relationship. Both polarities and viewpoints are necessary. Bateson called this added dimension *binocular vision*. The binocular view provides sharp focus and relief, while the monocular view is flat and one-dimensional. Since our own views of events are subjective, or monocular, we have difficulty seeing the comprehensive context.

Without a good friend to talk to, a caring mate, or a competent therapist, we stand little chance of getting outside of ourselves to investigate other points of view. In other words, we remain stuck in the subjective world, unable to appreciate the part in association with the larger whole.

As noted, without something to solve, we do not grow. But growth does not mean playing ping-pong as we move from one pole to the other. It means looking at the space in between the poles for signs of new life.

In their landmark book *Change* (1974), Watzlawick, Weakland, and Fisch explained that, "One of the most common fallacies about change is the conclusion that if something is bad, its opposite must of necessity be good" (p. 19).

It is counterintuitive to think the opposite action will produce the same result; yet it happens all the time. Movement to the opposite pole is a reflexive action instilled with hope, but devoid of awareness. It leaves no choice but to replicate the very patterns we are trying to avoid.

Common to the law of polarity, we unconsciously move in the opposite direction of what we are trying to escape. One pole activates the other. As long as we fail to negotiate the vast space in between, we will be condemned to repeat the patterns perpetuated upon us.

To change or not to change: Change is a natural part of life. Like a Heraclitean river, our relationships change all the time. Even though they may be familiar, they are never the same as when first established. They, and we, are never the same twice.

Accommodating to fluctuations in relationships, without stagnating, is the mark of a mature relationship. Accommodation does not mean putting up with or accepting the other person. It means changing in meaningful ways by adding new dimensions to the relationship.

It is easy to get trapped, become habituated to a certain type of relationship, often unaware of its life-sucking effect. Typical reasons for staying in such relationships include, doing it: (1) for the sake of the children; (2) out of convenience; (3) because it will cost too much to divorce, or; (4) because we have already been divorced and do not want our second or third marriage to fail as well.

The ability to stay in a loveless relationship is a double-edged sword. On one hand it speaks to incredible perseverance in the face of overwhelming obstacles. On the other hand, it is the inability to perceive the damaging effects such a decision has on the bigger picture.

This typical situation brings to mind the parable of the ever-adaptive frog placed in a pot of water on the stove. As the heat is turned up, the frog's ability to adjust to the increasing temperature demonstrates its adaptive capacity. As the water gets hotter, we marvel at how the frog's body temperature regulates to the increasingly hostile environment. Only when the frog boils to death, do we realize the bigger picture.

If we are unable to see the effects of our actions in the larger context, we lay prone to those effects appearing again. The frog parable is instructive to human relationships. We ask: How do we know whether we are adapting to healthy changes in the environment or simply boiling to death?

Multiple Levels Within Relationships

Surface and hidden levels: Consistent with the law of polarity, the attraction force is comprised of two levels, the surface and hidden. At the surface level, we find observable behavioral characteristics. At the hidden level of human functioning, we find the interior level not open to everyday observation. These two levels are similar to reading a text that has a deeper meaning beyond its surface content. On one level, the text tells a logical and detailed story. On a deeper level, hidden meanings are open to different interpretations and analyses.

As Heraclitus says in fragment fifteen, "Nature prefers to hide." There are hidden properties corresponding to observable phenomena. Even though we do not have direct access to the hidden level, we can see its effects everywhere, since the hidden level and the surface level coexist.

In psychology, the surface and hidden levels of human behavior are addressed by *systems theory* and *psychoanalytic theory*. Systems theory is a logical and sequential process focusing on reciprocity and shared responsibility within the context of the family or any other system. Psychoanalytic theory emphasizes the underlying process, personally charged and individually based. The hidden aspects underlying human behavior include unconscious wishes, internalizations, and repressed facts.

The interactive level of systems theory is visible and observable. It does not require interpretation or deep exploration because it can be seen through its interactions. In contrast, no one has ever seen an ego or an unconscious desire; we see manifestations of the ego or unconscious desires through their associated behavioral patterns.

Contrary to the systems view of family interaction where the whole is greater than the sum of its parts, in mysticism, the whole is in each part, allowing intimate connections to all levels above and below. We are constantly challenged to differentiate the part from the whole without losing connection to the bigger picture. Likewise, we are challenged to separate from our families without losing connection with them.

We struggle with this part to whole definition on every conceivable level because we are both part and whole, or what Wilber (1995) calls *part/wholes*. Without the whole we cannot define the part and without the part we cannot comprehend the whole.

In this regard, the human experience is one of ever deepening contexts of interaction. The hidden and surface layers coexist, but function at different frequencies. As with Bateson, Jung, von Bertalanffy, Levi-Strauss, as well as the ancient mystics Pythagoras and Heraclitus, one level of existence is intricately connected to the next, so the whole pattern can be seen in each of its parts. Although we do not experience the same circumstances more than once, we sense vague similarities among events because they are connected through an overall pattern.

Psychiatrist Edgar Levenson (1972) suggested that each moment of therapy contains the entire history of the client in present form. By paying attention to the moment or microstructure of a life, we have access to the entirety of the person's life, or macro structure. Whether we pay attention to the behavioral level or to the unconscious level, or to the present or the past, we have access to the entire history of the client in the moment. This is why a psychiatrist views a problem as a chemical imbalance, a family therapist views the same problem as a systemic issue, a psychodynamic therapist views it as an ego problem, and a physician views it as a medical problem. The entire pattern exists in whatever part is being examined. On every level of human functioning there is a distinct manifestation of the particular symptom because all levels are connected.

This part to whole relationship is the basis of the law of correspondence. It is also the foundation of the medieval classification system the *Doctrine of Signatures*, stipulating that each thing has its own personal identifier or signature revealing an entire pattern in each isolated part. The Doctrine of Signatures is steeped in mystical symbolism found in herbal medicine practice. Healers believed God had marked each thing with a sign corresponding to the treatment of specific illnesses. Just as the discerning therapist sifts through the language to perceive a pattern signified by a behavior, the ancient seer distilled an entire pattern from the shape of a single leaf.

Since the whole is reflected in the part, everything we perceive is the surface manifestation of a hidden pattern. This hidden pattern, along with the obvious physical appeal on the surface level, forms the basis for the attraction force. As we explore the law of polarity, we realize we are attracted on levels exceeding comprehension until we uncover the hidden patterns.

The karmic level: Since we are social animals, we need relationships to thrive emotionally. By attracting mates who resonate with our imagos, we set the conditions forcing us to deal with constrictive childhood internalizations. Without adequately understanding the connections between the surface and hidden levels, we naively reduce attractions to the surface level. Thus we are unprepared when unconscious patterns surface during the course of the relationship.

Human experience is based on growth and learning. If we do not move forward, we stagnate. We move forward by overcoming constraints. Just as one thing flows from another, one learning point leads to another. Our key relationships offer the greatest opportunities for growth.

In marriage, we take on the next sequential learning objective. Naively, we think we will marry, raise a family, and live happily ever after. We feel fooled when we discover how much hard work is required for relationships to thrive. We are shocked to learn marriage includes many more things than we thought.

The concept of marriage as work seems foreign because if we have to put a lot of effort into relationships, there must be something wrong with them. But all relationships require work to sustain themselves.

The sign of a good relationship is not the absence of conflict, but how the conflict is resolved. Conflict resolution takes hard work. This is where most relationships fail. When conflict appears, the partners move to opposite poles and entrench. This polar entrenchment locks relationships into rigid and predictable behavioral patterns, causing stagnation. The partners must move beyond constraining early internalizations and stop projecting them onto each other. In conflict resolution, the following three points are important:

- One pole activates another.

- Both poles represent a complete range along a certain spectrum.
- Spouses who argue without changing their style of interaction, only intensify the distance between the two poles.

Because our relationships require work, we have the opportunity to grow beyond confining family patterns internalized in childhood. The learning points are logical: to move to point B, we must resolve point A. If we ignore point A, it will reposition itself until we deal with it. We cannot move to point B without dealing with point A. If we move away from a problem, the problem will find us. Avoidance of personal issues is a primary reason relationships fall into predictable and repetitious patterns.

In the following example, Todd and Mary have a repetitive fight about responsibility. Mary wants Todd to pay more attention to the bills and budgetary concerns. Todd wants Mary to follow through on the things she says she will do. They both stockpile events and when one gets upset and confronts the other, the accumulated events come flying out. Mary has great ideas, but before following through with one plan, she generates five new ones. Compelled to finish the things Mary starts, Todd lets the budget slide. Since, he does not like the restriction of a budget, he enters into a tacit contract, agreeing to finish her projects if she consents to do the finances without him. Silent agreements such as this never last long since they are created out of avoidance.

Neither Todd nor Mary can grow without dealing with this persistent problem. Todd must learn how to be more fiscally responsible and Mary must learn how to follow through before she begins another project. These growth areas seem minor until family of origin influences are considered. Todd's father filed for bankruptcy twice and Mary's mother never completed college because of moving from city to city. These karmic family patterns were handed down to Todd and Mary. Todd has difficulty with money and Mary has difficulty staying on task.

The karmic relationship formed with Todd and Mary allows them to work through their previous levels of inherited constraint. If they do not adequately address their issue, it will reposition itself in front of them until it is resolved. Problems wait, staying with us until we resolve them.

Summary

To advance beyond the previous generations, we must overcome restrictive internalized childhood patterns. In close relationships, such as marriage, we resolve our personal patterns, repair the dualities of our earlier identifications and counter-identifications, and connect with our true selves. Basic concepts include the following:

- Attraction to others is based on the early childhood styles and parental patterns internalized as imagos.
- Because of our imagos, we choose partners with patterns identical to our parents or the opposite. They unknowingly reset our childhood patterns.
- Through the attraction of like and opposite imagos we attempt to resolve unfinished circumstances.
- Self-fulfilling prophesies occurs when we make selections based on our expectations.
- Observable behavioral characteristics are at the surface level of the attraction force.
- Unconscious wishes, internalizations, and repressed facts are the hidden aspects underlying human behavior.
- Connections between the surface and hidden levels allow us to understand unconscious patterns. For example, we shift to the opposite pole to resolve fears and anxieties resulting from previous attachments.
- Using the law of polarity, we realize we are drawn to partners on deep levels that make sense when we uncover the hidden patterns.
- Manifestations of a symptom can be seen at every level since all levels are connected.

Like life, relationships are dynamic and involve struggle. To become more complete in personality and spirit, we must reconcile opposite forces in our relationships. Such conflict resolution signifies good relationships.

Chapter Eight: Creating a Conscious Marriage

To be wise is one thing; to know the thought that directs all things through all things.

Heraclitus

Everything in life has a natural order and relationships are no exception. We marry for the right reasons, but the attraction to certain people guarantees childhood patterns will continue until resolved in adult relationships. Consequently, marriage can become a battleground, replete with arguing, withdrawal, and sarcasm, threatening its very existence. Although desirable, keeping the relationship viable is not the point. Sustaining a bad relationship gratifies only the masochist.

When we understand the dynamic nature of the attraction force, we cease blaming the shortcomings of others and realize we are drawn to mates in an attempt to free ourselves from childhood constraints. If current relationships fail and we learn from them, next relationships may exceed all expectations. We may look back on current failures with gratitude.

Spanish poet Antonio Machado (1983) captured the positive nature of negative experiences in the following poem:

Last night, as I was sleeping
I dreamed—marvelous error!—
that I had a beehive
here inside my heart.
And the golden bees
were making white combs
and sweet honey
from my old failures.

Past relationships will not be in vain once we realize there is something to *learn* from them, rather than dwelling on what was *wrong* with them. This chapter focuses on developing a conscious marriage by expanding beyond childhood constraints into more effective relationship styles.

Early Stages of Marriage

In adulthood, the ongoing differentiation and integration process begun in childhood is brought into marriage. Mahler's stages of child development can be applied to marriage. Consider the initial dreamlike merger of newlyweds, the symbiotic spousal dependency, followed by separation and individuation.

Just as children are challenged to separate from their mothers without losing love, couples face challenges as marital bliss gives way to individual differences. They must determine how to keep connected to each other without sacrificing personal identity. Balancing one life-affirming state with another is difficult for child and adult alike.

The paradox of being separated and connected at the same time is at the heart of mysticism and human life. Marriage poses the same question asked in mysticism and childhood: How do we maintain personal identity while integrating the larger system (in this case, the marriage) into our lives?

The answer lies in the creation of the conscious marriage. By analyzing the typical progression of marriage, we can identify the major challenges to developing a conscious marriage.

The honeymoon period: The honeymoon period of marriage is generally three months to three years long. During this time, there is a sense of wholeness and completion as each partner brings the missing pole to the other. This early stage produces its own momentum. A young relationship does not deal with keeping itself fresh and motivated since it is a self-sustaining system fueled by shared chemistry. This desire, sometimes experienced as a hunger, draws the partners together with such intensity, it spawned the cliché *love is blind.* They are so excited at the thought of seeing each other, touching each other, and sharing from their open hearts, they become blind to the initial attraction. They want the relationship so badly, they make allowances for behaviors they will not tolerate later.

Up to this point *relationship chemistry* provides the momentum. When the self-sustaining nature of relationship chemistry dwindles, the couple must rely on their own motivational impulses to keep the relationship going. This is when relationships can falter.

In the first stage of marriage, spouses bring their childhood patterns to form the larger pattern of the marriage. At first, these patterns converge in exciting ways. But this initial convergence is not a *conscious marriage* since the newness of the relationship—with all of its anticipation, arousal, and sexual tension—is generally so strong, it colors the thinking. There is nothing like a new relationship, because it feels like being mystically merged. The couple experiences again the wholeness and completion of the early maternal merger and the distant memory of the primordial connection to the universe. When the first marital stage ends, some people think the relationship has soured, when in reality it has simply matured.

Take the example of Jim and Alley, who fell in love only to discover that love alone could not sustain their marriage. When Jim married Alley, he was attracted to her free spirit and independence. He came from a previous marriage where his wife never made any decisions without his approval. Although he liked the control, he did not like carrying the burden of the relationship alone. After several years of marriage to Alley, Jim felt her independence signaled that she did not need him. Feeling alone again, he became insecure and began to scrutinize Alley's behavior, leaving her feeling constrained and resentful. The vicious cycle of *insecurity-scrutiny-resentment-distance* repeated until Jim and Alley became completely polarized. Relationship momentum was no longer carrying their marriage. For their relationship to survive, Jim and Alley had to produce the energy to move their marriage in a new direction. This marked the end of the honeymoon period. Jim and Alley had three clear choices: they could remain polarized and suck all the energy out of the relationship, they could divorce, or they could seek help to discover new ways of interacting.

The second stage of marriage: The second stage of marriage focuses on establishing partner roles and expectations and settling into routines. The partners are often developing careers, establishing a home, and raising children, leaving them with little time to focus on the relationship.

During the second stage of marriage there are no new emotional forces driving the marriage. When personal expectations are set and the marital roles are clearly defined, the marriage is at its most vulnerable point. Sex often becomes predictable and, in most cases, less exciting. Even comfortable routines seem like ruts. This is the time for assuming responsibility for the progress of the marriage. If the relationship matures partners experience personal growth within the marriage.

The second stage of marriage can also produce negativity: affairs occur, spouses feel older and unappealing, boredom creeps in, and the idea of working on the marriage seems out of place. Partners have already put a lot of energy into learning to be with each other.

Like exuberant, invincible adolescents, they never think the initial infatuation will end, but it does. Along with it goes the hope for eternal bliss. Once experienced, it is hard to settle for less than a mystical merger. So in the second stage of marriage, they are tempted to revisit their glory days by forming new romantic relationships. The lure of the affair, the younger woman or the more secure man, feed the imagination and spark feelings of being alive.

The second stage of marriage ends long after the sentiment of the new marriage wanes and partners settle into predictable routines. At this point, the couple is challenged to turn the relationship into a conscious one, rather than one that runs on the emotions of love, lust, desire, and the mystical union.

If unsuccessful, the couple may divorce or remain stuck in the second stage of marriage indefinitely, replaying their unhappy and unresolved scenarios. Or they may begin the third stage, the task of developing a conscious marriage.

The third stage of marriage—the conscious marriage: A conscious marriage is treated as a separate and distinct entity from the spouses. The partners realize the marriage needs its own definition, rules, structure, and identity. To thrive, it cannot perpetuate polarizing actions arising from anger, fear, jealousy and insecurity. It is cared for as if a living organism and not simply the result of two separate people doing their own things while being coupled to each other. To Whitaker (1978), this concept contained we-ness, an essential ingredient for a thriving marriage. When a marriage experiences a sense of "we," it becomes greater than the two people who created it.

The question for each spouse is: Will my behavior benefit the marriage? If the answer is no, the spouse must rethink the behavior. This question signals that the marriage has its own separate existence and each partner directs its destiny.

Unfortunately, many spouses represent their own individual positions and fail to see how they are contributing to the larger structure and outcome. According to Welwood (2000), "Whenever we solidify or identify with any position—exclusively arguing for closeness or space, separateness or togetherness, freedom or commitment—we can harm ourselves because we lose touch with the whole of what we are, in favor of one isolated part" (p. 244). Relationship consciousness is raised when the couple understands it takes binocular vision for the marriage to be successful.

As a marriage becomes more conscious, it also becomes more inclusive. In mysticism, the universe is *both* separate *and* connected as in marriage. It is an inclusive collaboration with room for both/and possibilities. Mysticism teaches us we are simultaneously individual and collective. But as we so often see in entrenched marriages, the collective of the marriage is forsaken for the individual's point of view.

Rather than the "you *or* me" rhetoric characterizing so many entrenched marriages, a conscious relationship becomes a "you *and* me" collaboration distinguished by a high level of reciprocity. You or me thinking implies either/or options, thus excluding one of the spouses. You and me thinking takes the whole marriage into consideration. The shift from you *or* me to you *and* me produces a different level of consciousness accommodating both spouses equally.

Wholeness requires the integration of two points of view, which eludes many modern-day marriages. Like the importance of polarity in unity, double description is key to understanding relationship dynamics. As in the wave-particle duality, conscious relationships embody the diversity of particles and the unity of waves in its structure.

In *either/or* and *right/wrong* paradigms, we do not embrace the notion that people can be both right and wrong at the same time. Having mental models of the world, we make situations fit particular frames of reference creating self-fulfilling prophecies. In the process, we overlook, discount, or pay selective attention to divergent views. We may spend a lot of time arguing over single interpretations rather than engaging in meaningful dialogues to explain particular views. "Real dialogue," says McKee (2003), "depends on us being passionately committed to our own world, and simultaneously, passionately interested in other worlds" (p. 404). Holding divergent positions simultaneously—your own position as well your partner's—without giving privilege to one over the other, is an essential challenge in the developmental cycle of a conscious marriage.

Family of Origin Influences

A precursor to creating a conscious marriage is the awareness of expectations resulting from family of origin influences. Expectations of marital functioning and managing conflict result from childhood experiences of parental interactions.

Children take in the environment as if watching a movie and, with repetition, it becomes unconsciously internalized. We may not realize these images are incorporated in our mental models until we marry and suddenly begin to act like our parents. In childhood, we create mental models for marriage, what it should and should not be. As stated, once internalized, these models remain static, never changing even as we continue to grow older.

The internalization of family of origin patterns includes parental norms and relationship styles. I have seen many couples live together for a long time without having any rigid expectations until they marry. The finality of the marital contract produces an instant new role, husband or wife. Once role-bound, they become role defined, unconsciously turning to the mental models internalized from their parents. These unconscious impulses from family of origin influences must be clarified to produce a conscious marriage.

The Three Domains

Three major domains must be taken into consideration for a marriage to become conscious: the work domain, the home domain, and the shared domain.

The work domain: In traditional families, the husband controls the work domain, that is, he leaves the home and goes to another domain where he stays for most of the day doing his job. The money he earns is used to run the household, another domain, which is under the control of the wife.

The home domain: Typically, the wife has the responsibility of running the household, including raising the children, paying the bills, and scheduling events for family members. In such marriages, there are two businesses: earning money and running the home.

The shared domain: There is usually little agreement in this domain. When the husband comes home from work, he is actually returning to his wife's domain. Once inside the home, it is his domain as well. The shared domain needs to be identified so the husband does not feel like he is *helping* his wife when, in effect, she is waiting for him to take charge. A typical polar opposition occurs when the husband returns home from work and thinks his work is finished. The wife, who has been working all day, now has the additional chore of taking care of her husband.

Although the above scenario may not depict today's family, a study by Hochschild (1989) concludes that in typical two income families, household tasks default to the woman. The shared domain is seen as the woman's domain whether she is working or not.

One explanation for the unequal distribution of household chores is that many contemporary women have mothers who did not participate in the work force. Consequently, they have no mental model for balancing the competing demands of work and family life.

In a conscious marriage, the household tasks do not simply default to the woman. As is often the case, the man's typical tasks, such as exterior house maintenance or car maintenance, occur infrequently compared to the woman's everyday tasks of food shopping, cooking, cleaning, and child rearing. Inside the home, the man may vacuum on a weekly basis, while the woman changes diapers, washes clothes, and keeps the house in order several times a day. Typically, the husband wants to help out the wife without realizing the house is a shared domain. When the couple consciously looks at household ownership, they negotiate responsibilities and the marriage takes on a more balanced and cooperative atmosphere.

Questionnaire for Creating a Conscious Marriage

The three stages of marriage, family of origin influences, and the three major domains are some of the challenges couples face in developing a conscious marriage. The questions below will help you build a strong framework for developing a conscious marriage by: (1) determining the influence of your family of origin on your choice of mate, (2) identifying the individual behavior patterns you bring to the marriage, and (3) revealing how you treat your personal and shared domain so you can expand beyond the constraints you internalized as a child.

Because mental models from childhood are unconsciously projected into relationships, we must come to terms with family of origin influences to create the marriages we desire.

The first set of questions relate to three categories central to all marriages: conflict resolution, money, and affection. Answer the questions to identify the effects family of origin have on you. Then, determine how your answers compare to your current personality style. Do you take the same or opposite positions as your parents?

1. **What were you taught about conflict resolution in your family?**
   a. Did your parents fight openly with each other?
   b. How loud or aggressive were they?
   c. How would fights come to an end?
   d. Would one parent always give in?

2. **How affectionate were your parents with each other?**
   a. Did you see open displays of affection?
   b. How did your parents show affection?
   c. How did you know that they loved each other?
   d. Did they withhold affection as punishment?

3. **How were the finances handled?**
   a. Did your parents fight about money?
   b. Was there enough money?
   c. Who earned the money?
   d. Who controlled the money?
   e. How was money used?, i.e., for reward, co   ⁀ion
      ego gratification.

What are your individual characteristics? As we internalize parental qualities and traits, we get stuck on one pole. Thus, we must explore the middle ground to produce balance in our lives.

Individual traits fall on a continuum of polarities. Using the list of polarities below, underline the trait in each set that best describes you in one color and underline those describing each parent in two other colors. This color-coding will allow you to discover the areas in which you identify and counter-identify with each parent. Also, the exercise will help reveal your parents' symmetrical and complementary areas. Try not to view each set of polarities as fixed, but as attributes you display more often than not.

Strong – Weak	Deep – Superficial
Exciting – Boring	Bright – Dull
Courageous – Fearful	Ambitious – Complacent
Anxious – Calm	Generous – Withholding
Strict – Lenient	Passive – Aggressive
Rigid – Chaotic	Stable – Changeable
Engaged – Peripheral	Authoritarian – Permissive
Happy – Sad	Extrovert – Introvert
Blaming – Accepting blame	Optimistic – Pessimistic
Warm – Cold	Dominant – Submissive
Rejecting – Accepting	Emotional – Unemotional
In control – Out of control	Loud – Soft
Responsible – Irresponsible	Available – Unavailable

Talkative – Quiet	Encouraging – Discouraging
Curious – Not interested	Impulsive – Cautious
Receptive – Closed	Intuitive – Reasoning
Logical – Illogical	Rational – Irrational
Plays it safe – Takes risks	Eccentric – Conventional
Takes charge – Defers	Affectionate – Contained

What do you expect from marriage? The mental model for marriage is set early in life by our parents. So, each of us must ask: What mental model of marriage have I incorporated from my parents? Below are some additional questions. The answers will give you a better idea of what to expect in your own marriage.

- How did your parents treat each other?
- What roles did they assume?
- Were they happy in their roles?
- What elements of their marriage do you want to keep?
- What elements of their marriage do you want to eliminate?

How do you treat the shared domain? The shared domain occurs when both partners are in the home. It is essential to identify when this occurs and how to treat it. Because the shared domain generally defaults to the wife, it is important for the husband to identify his intended areas of ownership and his wife's expectations regarding his ownership areas.

How do you treat your personal domain? Since the marriage is a combination of a shared domain, as well as two individual domains, each partner needs to describe a personal domain, what occurs within it, and the expectation of the other in the personal domain.

What are you willing to do to make the marriage work? Make a detailed list of what you are willing to do to make the marriage work.

This begins defining the *we* of marriage. Such information exchange increases mutuality, shows respect for the other person, promotes personal responsibility, heightens each partner's initiative, and demonstrates the ability to compromise for the sake of the relationship.

Summary

In serious adult relationships, such as marriage, we are drawn to mates in an attempt to free ourselves from childhood constraints. But just as in childhood, we need to learn how to maintain personal identity while integrating marriage into our lives. This chapter focused on the stages of marriage and the underlying forces to overcome in creating the conscious marriage. Major concepts include the following:

- Marriage goes through predictable stages.
- During the honeymoon period, there is a natural momentum resulting from the sense of wholeness and completion each partner brings to the other, representing the missing pole in their lives. This stage is driven by love, lust, desire, and the effects of the mystical union.
- Once the honeymoon is over, spouses unconsciously draw on mental models of parental relationships internalized during childhood to determine their behaviors.
- To develop the conscious marriage, these unconscious impulses from family of origin influences need to be identified and resolved.
- A conscious marriage results in a sense of *we* where the relationship becomes greater than the two people who created it.
- The work, the home, and the shared domains must be handled in a conscious manner. The shared domain requires the greatest attention and provides an arena for negotiating responsibilities and creating a balanced and cooperative atmosphere.

A conscious marriage is built on mutuality, respect, and most of all, awareness. To create a conscious marriage, we need to recognize how childhood patterns influence our adult relationships and how our mates fit into the personal patterns we endeavor to transcend.

Chapter Nine: Healing the Eternal Split in Adult Relationships

Do not act and speak as if asleep.
Heraclitus

Marriages typically resist change. But without change, relationships tend to stagnate. Replacing either/or thinking with both/and thinking is a first step toward balancing individual and collective polarities in marriage. Either/or thinking offers the spouses only two options under stress, either a spouse is right or a spouse is wrong. It is easy to see how the either/or proposition sets up a never-ending loop of accusations and defensiveness in the life cycle of a marriage.

The *I'm right, you're wrong* mentality so prevalent in today's culture is indicative of the polar splits we must heal to advance our relationships. In complementary and symmetrical marriages, we choose mates who reactivate our unresolved childhood patterns and then entrench against them as targets of denial. The solution to these habitual overreactions is to learn to *interact* in new ways, instead of *reacting* in reflexive, ineffective, and outdated ways.

You're Both Right/You're Both Wrong

Using modern-day mysticism to unify couples: Because mysticism allows for two distinct points of view in a single system, we can eliminate the one-sided right/wrong thinking characterizing so many relationships by acknowledging that two people can be right and wrong at the same time. By doing so, we can create better connections.

In marriage, two people share the boundaries of one common unit, so there are always two different opinions. With two different views it is easy for marriages to descend into either/or thinking as each spouse fights for identity space by denying the reality of the partner. We identify and separate ourselves by underscoring our differences with other people, especially our spouses. In the process, the marriage suf

According to the law of polarity, no one is right or v
there is no right and wrong in the universe, only multiple
singular source. In a conscious marriage there are no '

answers, no me versus you, no correct versus incorrect, just different perceptions. Thus, spouses can be right and wrong at the same time. In entrenched marriages the opposite occurs. Spouses become rigid in their opinions leaving little room for agreement.

The approach I systematized, called *you're both right/you're both wrong,* shows how two contradictory views can co-exist in a relationship. It fosters individuality and connection and promotes unified partnerships consistent with the law of polarity.

The following vignette reveals the schisms typical of complementary couples and shows how the you're both right/you're both wrong approach heals polar splits.

Erik and Sara: When Erik and Sara came to therapy, they were entrenched in their respective positions. Erik felt Sara was negative about everything and Sara felt Erik was avoidant and unresponsive. Although Sara and Erik had correct perceptions of each other's behavior, the intensity of their reactions resulted from family of origin influences. Together, they fell into old patterns and then blamed each other for their own constraints.

From our limited, monocular view of the world, we defend our positions by projecting our inadequacies onto other people—our bosses, family members, children, or spouses—who occupy the opposite poles. Then we entrench in our own positions until our communication patterns look like long redundant loops of never ending accusations, attacks, and defensive posturing.

Sara was correct that Erik was avoidant and unresponsive, but incorrect that his behavior was the sole cause of her anger. Her anger stemmed from patterns predating the marriage. Because her family was loud and boisterous, she saw any sign of withdrawal or disengagement as a personal rejection. When Erik no longer gave her quiet assurance, she felt rejected and reverted to her childhood behavior, becoming loud and aggressive.

Erik was correct about Sara's negativity, but wrong in assuming it was caused by his withdrawal. When Erik was a child he withdrew when his father belittled him. If Sara became aggressive and negative, he withdrew as in his childhood. Sara felt arguing was the only way to engage Erik, even though he dealt with conflict by withdrawing. Erik and Sara reacted to each other without taking responsibility for their own family karmas. With the moral superiority and self-righteousness of their monocular visions, they blamed each other for personal behaviors.

Psycho-education: The you're both right/you're both wrong intervention shows how partners unconsciously use the other's reactions as excuses for their own behaviors. Because Sara internalized her family's chaotic and negative style, her choice of Erik for a spouse, with his laid-back attitude, was logical. As the marriage matured, Sara viewed Erik's laid-back attitude as indifference, triggering her latent insecurities. To move forward, she had to deal with her insecurities.

Erik identified with his mother, who had a mild-mannered exterior. He internalized his father's negativity, thereby expecting people to be critical of him. When he met Sara, he felt safe and secure with her take-charge attitude, but when the strength of her personality overwhelmed him, he felt criticized. Although Erik counter-identified with his father, he married a woman having his father's behavioral style. Consequently, he assumed his mother's role and became passive, expecting Sara to take care of him. To move forward, Erik had to deal with his passivity.

After learning about their patterns, issues, and themes, Erik and Sara understood their assertions about each other. But their claims were limited in scope. By learning that people seek like or opposite patterns in an unconscious attempt to re-create family of origin issues, Erik and Sara understood they had to confront their personal constraints within the marriage to move ahead.

This comprehensive notion of marriage gives voice to the unconscious forces bringing people together in the hope of creating greater wholeness. Using the you're both right/you're both wrong approach with Erik and Sara was more than a positive reframe of their situation. It was true that they were both right and both wrong, in their assessment of the situation. Now they could reclaim power and maintain control while expanding their mental models to allow for the other's point of view.

Undoing projection and blame: Projection allows us to expose our inner selves to the world so we see the whole picture. It is the psyche's natural means of ridding itself of unpleasant internalizations.

Like Erik and Sara, if we believe a projection is the entire truth, we rob ourselves of valuable opportunities for personal growth. Unquestionably, many projections in relationships contain blame. When we blame others, we become angry and self-righteous because we see them as the cause of our discontent. May (1969) said, "Blaming the enemy implies that the enemy has the freedom to chose and act, not ourselves and we can only react to him" (p.193).

By projecting our blame we relinquish power. Similarly, when we blame ourselves, we become depressed and self-esteem suffers; we feel we cannot do anything right. Instead of projecting energy outside, we keep it internalized, leaving us guilty, bereft of hope, and depressed. In an unconscious marriage, projection can result in getting rid of the spouse instead of self-unification.

"If Sara wasn't so emotional," or "If Erik was more assertive," were common complaints from Erik and Sara. Relationships break down under the weight of such self-indulgent thinking. When blame and accusations take over a marriage, each partner waits for the other to admit fault and take corrective measures. Fault can never be admitted under these conditions, since it would mean giving in to the other person, something entrenched partners will not do. What they really want is recognition. Ironically, in entrenched couples, recognition is the very thing withheld.

Using the both right/both wrong model has helped many individuals and couples undo projections and self-blame. They see the elements of truth in both positions and understand that both positions are needed to understand the complete story. This approach is validating and legitimate and breaks the recursive loop. Partners can no longer entrench after knowing their assertions are correct, but incomplete.

Listening to Erik, I could conclude Sara was irrational and on edge all the time. Listening to Sara, I could think Erik was meek and passively sabotaging the marriage. Sara realized she was correct about Erik's passivity, but incorrect about it being the only cause for her intense reaction. Erik learned he was correct about Sara's negativity, but incorrect about blaming her for his withdrawal. Thus, they both gained insight as to how their own karmic family issues were reset in their marriage. To succeed, they both had to take responsibility.

Process versus content: The you're both right/you're both wrong intervention can be used on one or more communication levels, for example, content and process. At the content level, verbal information is relayed back and forth; at the process level, emotional factors are communicated.

Many times one partner will not listen to what the other has to say because of the way the content is communicated. For example, Erik had a terrible time listening to Sara because of her emotional tone. She had legitimate things to say, but her tone overshadowed the content. Instead of paying attention to what Sara said, Erik attended to how she said it. Consequently, Sara never felt she was heard, making her speak even more emphatically.

This classic form of miscommunication brings us back to the redundant loop. Sara became frustrated because Erik was not listening to her and Erik withdrew because of Sara's tone. While Sara was focusing on the content, Erik was focusing on the process.

Instead of dealing with one level at a time, they complicated the communication by using the content level to address the process level and vice versa. They were both unconsciously colluding to maintain their habitual communication styles. Erik allowed Sara to take over by withdrawing and Sara compelled Erik to be quiet with her tone. Sara yelled, just like her family, and Erik cowered as he did in childhood. They were stuck in this dynamic, using old, ineffective responses to address marital issues.

The you're both right/you're both wrong intervention was effective in eliminating this redundant loop because Eric and Sara were both right and wrong in their assertions. Sara's tone did push Erik away and Erik's withdrawal did elicit an intense response from Sara. Since they were both addressing one level of communication with unfit responses, they were also both wrong. To communicate effectively, Erik needed to address Sara's content and Sara needed to address Erik's feelings about her treatment of him. The redundant loop was broken when they focused on one pole at a time, addressing either the emotional tone or the content, rather than responding to each other from opposite poles.

Other Polarity-based Techniques and Interventions

The use of paradox: Polar shifting occurs when pressure is placed on one pole causing a compensatory shift to the opposite pole to maintain the relationship balance. For example, when my son was five years old, I could guarantee he would kiss me goodnight by insisting he not do it. My son asserted his independence by doing the opposite of the request, even if it meant doing what I wanted.

This common game is consistent with the law of polarity and is based on principles of reverse psychology and paradoxical interventions. My son and I both did the right thing, even though it seemed I tricked him. Once he grew up, however, he had to play the game differently. If he opposed me, or anyone in a position of authority, he would not be practicing independence; he would be oppositional. There is no growth in being oppositional as an adult.

As a strategy, polar shifting reduces tension and allows more adaptive behaviors to emerge. But in everyday life, we instinctively do the opposite of the expected, without awareness of the consequences. This natural inclination toward polar shifting is the basis of many paradoxical interventions, most notably those in Haley's (1976) strategic approach, in the Milan group's (Selvini Palazzoli, Boscolo, Cecchin, & Prata, 1974) use of positive connotation, and in the Mental Research Institute's (Watzlawick, Beavin, & Jackson, 1967) brief therapy model of prescribing the symptom.

Because Erik and Sara's opposition was so clear, it was possible to shift their behaviors using a paradoxical intervention. In their interactions, Erik elicited Sara's negative response or he withdrew. To stop this redundant loop, I suggested that every time he elicited Sara's negative response, he was asking her to beat him over the head as his father did. Eric required it as proof of his father's love. Consequently, Erik unconsciously made sure Sara was angry with him so he would feel loved.

Sara was easily seduced into anger and yelling because it was the only proof that her family cared about her. By yelling at Erik, she was showing she cared in the only way she knew how. When I reframed Sara's angry response to Erik as her way of making love to him, it was no longer possible for them to fight without thinking it was a substitute for their mutual unexpressed love and affection. If they accepted this reframing, they would add a new level of affection to their relationship. If they rejected it, they would have to deal with their unexpressed affection every time they got into a negative communication loop. In either case, their behavior would change.

Doing something uncommon rather than more of the same: It takes an uncommon act to break a pattern since behavior is deep-seated. In doing the uncommon, we can break repetitive patterns, since uncommon behaviors shift us to opposite poles. The uncommon interrupts patterns created through the usual responses to situations.

An uncommon act is something that should be done but has been put off. Ask yourself this question: If I do x what would the result be? If the result is something you can predict and the outcome is unsatisfying, than x is the repetitive behavior and not the uncommon behavior. Now ask yourself what the opposite behavior would be. For instance, if you generally wait for people to phone you, an uncommon behavior would be to reach out first. Or if you are naturally thrifty, an uncommon behavior would be to become more generous.

For Sara to feel positive self-esteem, she would have to get her emotional needs met in another area of her life, reducing the pressure on the relationship to be the source of her well being. Since she only knew how to define herself in the context of a chaotic and boisterous family, it would be uncommon to break out of that pattern and find self worth in another arena. For Erik, attending an assertiveness training class to become proactive would be an uncommon behavior.

Uncommon acts break negative cycles of behavior. It is simple to identify an uncommon act—it is the opposite of what we naturally do— and it is the hardest thing for us to do. For example, in an argument involving a husband's excuse for visiting a strip club, the wife's emotions are escalating out of control as he rationalizes his actions. When he says the friend driving wanted to go and he could not say "no," she explodes. Her explosion was predictable. The uncommon act, however, would have changed the entire dynamic. She could have counted to ten and calmed herself down or walked away and come back to the situation when cooler heads prevailed. A contrary action requires uncommon strength and discipline when we are emotionally charged.

The simplest things are the deepest things and they are not necessarily easy.

The 90/10 rule: According to the 90/10 formula, couples agree on 90 percent of the issues, but spend 90 percent of the time arguing over the 10 percent they disagree about. The 90/10 inversion occurs because couples focus on what activates them, not on the harmonious aspects.

In Eric and Sara's marriage, Eric's tendency to withdraw activated Sara, who viewed it as an act of aggression against her and lashed out. There were times when Eric withdrew and Sara did not lash out at all. For instance, Eric often retreated to work in his woodshop. Because there were no interactive variables attached to the wood shop, Sara did not react. At these times, she associated his withdrawal to his calm personality style and enjoyed the peacefulness without thinking to tell him his quiet demeanor made the house more pleasant. When he withdrew as a result of an interaction, her emotions escalated. She reverted to the internalized family behaviors, viewing Eric's withdrawal as inconsistent with the expected behavior during disagreements. She expected heated engagements, but got passive withdrawals. Given the inconsistency between her mental model and the actual situation, Sara tried to pull Eric into her personal schema, creating total emotional chaos. When activated by Eric, Sara viewed him as passive-aggressive; when not activated she saw him as calm and peaceful. Consequently, the couple fought when activated and took each other for granted when things went well.

You would never know by their interactions, but Sara and Eric agreed on many things. They liked the same food, movies, television shows, humor, books, and shared the same morals and religious beliefs. Yet they rarely interacted around these agreements in loving ways. They took them for granted, giving them little attention because there was no heat.

One way to change the interactions is to spend more time talking about areas of agreement. This minor shift in relationship dynamics dramatically reduces the percentage of time couples fight relative to the percentage of time they interact. They may still fight as much as before, but they do so within a context of more positive interactions. By addition, rather than subtraction, their relationship will become more stable.

If Eric and Sara change the percentage of time they fight with each other by increasing the amount of time they positively interact, their marriage will reach a higher level of organization. If the 90/10 percentage between Eric and Sara moves to a 50/50 percentage, the result will be less polarization and more stability in their marriage.

Summary

This chapter focused on how to mitigate marital rifts caused by the internal splits transferred from childhood and projected onto the spouse. Realizing projection is a natural process, we can become less defensive about our positions and work toward better connections in our relationships. Major concepts include the following:

- In complementary and symmetrical marriages, one pole activates the other, but both poles are required for partners to have a total picture of the situation.
- Consistent with the law of polarity, no one is right or wrong since there is no right and wrong in the universe.
- The you're both right/you're both wrong intervention can be used for both content and process communications, addressing the message itself and the emotional tone of the message.
- Since internalized behavior is instinctive, it takes an uncommon act to break a pattern. In polarized situations, taking the opposite behavior is uncommon. Taking such action requires great strength and discipline.
- According to the 90/10 formula, couples agree on 90 percent of the issues, but spend 90 percent of the time fighting over the 10 percent disagreement areas.
- An easy way to change the interactions is to spend more time talking about areas of agreement. Changing the 90/10 to a 50/50 percentage, results in less polarization and more stable relationships.

Couples find balance when they are simultaneously separate/connected, right/wrong, and part/whole, thus working within the universal principles of mysticism. Viewed holistically, marriage is one complete unit of both/and possibilities, promoting harmony and collaboration over division. By resolving family of origin issues and polar entrenchments, we move toward the goal of developing the conscious marriage.

Section Three: Using Mystical Principles to Develop the True Self

Chapter Ten: Life, Death, and Transcendence

*They do not understand how being
in conflict it still agrees with itself;
there is an opposing coherence, as
in the tensions of the bow and the
lyre.*

Heraclitus

The previous section showed how the principles of mysticism impact personality development, repetitive behavior patterns, choice of mate, and the development of a conscious marriage. This section addresses transcendence and the development of the true self. We achieve higher levels of consciousness and develop our true selves by extending beyond the constraints of family of origin influences. Because transcendence has a physical correlation and practical counterpart in everyday life, mysticism is broadened to include ordinary states.

Our Connection to the Greater Whole

Three spheres of influence: According to the principles of mysticism, there is always a logical harmony between and within the layers of every system. This consistency is found in the contrasting work of William James and Sigmund Freud. James (1909), considered the father of psychology in America, wrote, "Our lives are like islands in the sea within a continuum of cosmic consciousness." He believed the fences we build around our identities limiting our experiences have weak spots, allowing "influences from beyond." These "leakages" provide an ultimate connection to a greater source.

James's notion of a restricted existence within a larger context is like Freud's theory of the unconscious mind. For Freud, the conscious mind and unconscious drives form one unit; for James the conscious mind and superconsciousness form one unit. For each, a necessary context is withheld from normal functioning, mitigating the connection to the greater whole. Freud and James searched for unity and found it, Freud by looking into a person's psyche and James by looking outside the psyche.

Freud and James identified three spheres of existence: the unconscious, the conscious, and the superconscious, each being independent within the context of a larger sphere of existence. Awareness of a larger connection occurs when there is leakage through the boundary walling one sphere from the other. Freud's boundary was the unconscious mind, where hidden drives and motivations were kept from interfering with conscious life. For James, the conscious life was the boundary keeping out the superconscious, where phenomena go beyond ego boundaries.

Both Freud and James created a nested system from the unconscious mind, to conscious awareness, to superconsciousness. Freud, with the eye of a scientist, and James, with the eye of a metaphysician, established similar theories about walled off existences and leakages. They understood how the circumscribed life becomes more expansive through the integration of spheres outside of conscious awareness.

The struggle to expand awareness and to integrate larger spheres of influence results in profound questions about life. Where did we come from? Did we have previous lives? Where will we go? Is there an afterlife?

From entrance to exit, we are defined by the polarities of birth and death. The inevitability of death is as mystical as the miracle of birth. It is as if we leak into and then leak out of the human sphere of existence. In his poem *Riders*, Robert Frost (1995) encouraged us to look at birth and death with less ego and more spirit.

> What is this talked-of mystery of birth
> But being mounted bareback on the earth?
> We can just see the infant up astride,
> His small fist buried in the bushy hide.

The union of space and time: Metaphysical speculation about death is generally left to religious studies. But if we are not theologically inclined, we miss the connection between the mysterious and the obvious, the spiritual and the physical. Esteemed scholar, Abraham Heschel (1951) said life is eternal because it belongs to the world of time, a world known to us through the physical space between birth and death. Since we are bound to the physical world by our senses, we have limited knowledge of existence outside our own physical space. "When we learn to understand that it is the spatial things that are constantly running out," Heschel said, "we realize that time is that which never expires, that it is the world of space which is rolling through the infinite expanse of time" (p. 97). In Herschel's space-time duality, time is expressed through the physical nature of space and human beings become receptacles of space and time. Analyzing Heschel's philosophy, we see life as the embodiment of body and soul. It is composed of seen, quantified, and studied elements as well as unseen and philosophical aspects left to human speculation.

Borges (1999), a master at putting the language of the universe into words, said, "My life is located in space, and the chiming of unanimous clocks punctuates my duration in time" (p. 7). Time and space dance together like the finite and the infinite, as time gives space its vitality and space gives time its outlet. Together they provide a physical existence and a spiritual connection for human beings.

In the Western world, the duality between the physical and metaphysical is submitted to the rigors of formal, quantifiable verification. If we can scientifically prove the things held in awe, we assume we will be safe from the unknown. So we create theories to satisfy our infinite desire to know.

Klein (1923) termed this *the epistemophilic instinct*. Rather than seeing space and time as two contrasting and indispensable sides of the same coin, we become polarized trying to prove our existence. Thus, we take the *meta* out of *metaphysics*. Once science has proven the existence of something, it becomes part of standard knowledge and we forget it once held metaphysical status.

Metaphysics fuels the thirst for physics because life demands the unfolding of the unknown into the known. The expression of infinity in our lives is the never-ending wealth of knowledge inspiring us. "The human heart seeks the infinite," wrote Tillich (1999), "because that is where the finite want to rest" (p. 19). Perhaps a grand unified theory has eluded us, because if we establish a formula explaining everything, we will lose polar tension and become God, rather than contemplate God.

When people die, we come face to face with time, since the physical body time inhabited is no longer there. As we stand at the threshold of the next world, a world the dying have just entered, we are struck numb.

The experience of death forces us to question life, to feel deeply, and to have faith. "Death is inside the bones," Neruda wrote (1993), "like a barking where there are no dogs." Death defies logic; yet without it, life would have no meaning. To experience death is to question life. It is as if we are laid before the altar of the afterworld and asked to suspend judgment to consider heaven's existence. As we grieve, we sense death, standing like a sentry at the edge of life, making sure no one peeks behind the veil. We are left to wonder: Is there transcendence? Death summons us to question the physical and consider the metaphysical.

Transcendence: Surpassing Primary Constraints

We are born wrapped in the limiting patterns of preceding generations, but unrestricted in the ability to transcend them. Childhood provides a limited view, since we can go back only as far as our parents. We cannot see into nonlocal events. The traditional psychological approach negates the mystics' view of time's endless influence. Popularized by Plato, the mystical concept of endless time found its way into every worldview, justifying the timelessness of the spirit or soul.

In mysticism, karma is the effect of one lifetime on the next, similar to ego psychology wherein the process of internalization is the influence of one generation on the next. Regardless of view, the task remains the same—to transcend the inherent limitations of personality structure. Since it is natural to be born into the limitations of parents, there is nothing to undo, just more things to do. This is true of karma and psychology. Working through karma means transcending personal constraints. In transcending personal constraints, each of us takes sole responsibility.

So we are left to wonder: At what point do we become greater than our parents? At what point do we transcend them and their limitations? Transcendence does not mean a spiritual leap to enlightenment. Rather it is a step beyond primary constraints.

Wrapped in preceding generational limitations, we are resolved to transcend them. No measure of money or fame will equal the satisfaction gained from controlling our own destinies instead of acting out the unmet needs of restrictive historical patterns. Transcendence is not easy, but we take on the challenge one way or another. Each of us struggles with the legacy every day as we endeavor not to get trapped in life's petty details.

In mysticism, the whole organizes the part, guaranteeing we will carry our parents, and our parent's parents, within as part of the collective family history. In the absence of their presence, we have internalized their voices. As adults, we no longer have to adhere to the childhood controls, but they reside within us nonetheless.

Awareness, the first principle of mysticism, is the first intervention toward transcendence. To transcend these internal limitations we must inventory how we are like and unlike our parents. By discovering the identified and counter-identified parental internalizations, we approach an integrated midpoint rather than act or react instinctively along polar lines.

Becker (1973) asked, "How does one transcend himself? How does he open himself up to new possibility?" His answer: "By realizing the truth of his situation. By dispelling the lie of his character, by breaking his spirit out of its conditioned prison" (p. 86). Becker termed our comfortable actions *the conditioned prison*. Our conditioned responses keep our true selves hidden.

According to Kierkegaard, the more comfortable people are, the less adjusted they become. To be comfortable is to live within the habitual restriction of the false self, without stretching out into new territories. Living within the comfort zone, we do not experience anxiety. We stay within character structure defenses instead of stepping out into new and different experiences. We stop taking risks and live safe, but circumscribed lives.

The false self results from unconsciously identifying and counter-identifying with our parents. Aptly named, the false self gives a false sense of identity and security. We do not realize we can move beyond the restrictions of this unconscious process into a more conscious identity space.

True identity comes from *conscious intent* and uncovering a unique destiny. Conscious intent requires work and energy to move us into new areas and behaviors.

- To be *conscious* is to be aware of hidden motivations and the contexts within.
- *Intent* is the direction we take after becoming conscious.

- *Conscious intent* is the act of positive creation.

Conscious intent is the knowledge that we can do whatever we want followed by taking the required action.

Steps to Transcendence

To be free we must realize that we can do whatever we want; no one is holding us back and our actions are our own. We have free will. But to move forward, we have to transcend constraining generational patterns. To become whole, we need to be aware of how polarities determine behavior patterns and provide the basis for identity. As we learn to transcend polar restrictions identity formation advances from the pole of *I can't* to *I can*. By learning how to move beyond polar identifications we extend ourselves into new ranges of life. To this end, I have developed six guiding principles consistent with the concepts outlined thus far.

Principle One: Karma is not just for mystics; it is everywhere. Taken from the Sanskrit word samsara, meaning cycle of life, karma came to signify to the ancient Greeks the debts from previous actions needing resolution to move forward. The key word in defining karma is *action*. Whether we take responsibility for past behavior or not, nothing changes unless we institute new actions.

Ideally, each generation transcends the previous one in a natural order, leaving the world a better place. With karma being the effect of one action upon another, we can see the family of origin effects and their karmic influences. Since our parents cannot *not* influence us, we carry their patterns within us. Because we strive to be free of such effects, we institute new cause and effect patterns. Through *conscious intent* we change our former karmic patterns and create a future free of past restrictions.

Principle Two: Awareness is an intervention. Awareness, the most mystical gift of unity, is the act of creation. The more we are aware terns and restrictions, the more options we have. Awareness is the althy life. If we are unaware of something, we cannot change omes through self-reflection, the ability to see what we otional objectivity. If we do not use awareness to its fullest capacity, we impose unnecessary restrictions upon ourselves. Through self-reflection, we see how individual situations are connected to larger patterns traced to early parental identifications and counter-identifications. Awareness of cause and effect patterns helps us deal with childhood karma. Continuing to react from old models, we carry our parent's limitations into adulthood and into the lives of our children. Without awareness, we pass down the same karma to future generations. To be true pioneers, we must transcend these limitations and make our marks on the world.

Principle Three: Do not wait for the universe to get your attention; you will not like its methods. We seem to wait for better times to do the things we should do immediately. We wait so long, life sometimes hits us over our heads to get our attention. This can happen through a relationship breakup, an illness, or the loss of a job. Then we realize we should have taken action long ago. The more we procrastinate the more life pushes us in directions to get our attention; into depression, bad relationships, bad timing, or just plain bad luck. Why wait for such inducements when we have all the tools we need? Do we really need a medical problem to cause us to lose weight or an affair to address long-standing marital issues? If we are too passive, life will deliver the decisive blow.

The equation *simple = deep, not easy* shows that the action required to change a pattern is undermined by inertia. The required action is simple to recognize, but difficult to complete, resulting in false starts, half-hearted attempts, and rationalizations for putting off until tomorrow what is difficult today. Eventually, we take action and move forward. So why wait? Life is the greatest teacher, but are we life's best students? What is life trying to say? How is life treating us? When does life support us and when does it let us down? By paying attention to how life treats us, we know the right and wrong ways to live.

Principle Four: Do not live defensively. In living defensively, we protect against something happening rather than taking normal risks. Consider three primary consequences to living defensively: (1) there is no forward movement, which causes relationships to become static, even if peaceful; (2) by protecting against something negative happening, we live in our future projections rather than living in the moment, and; (3) the control over our lives, and ultimately the power we have to control our lives, lies outside of us, in the hands of whatever we are defending against. We are reactive rather than proactive.

Living defensively is an attempt to avoid conflict by protecting against pain-causing events. To protect against the recurrence of certain events, like personal failures or rejection, we have to be vigilant not to reproduce those outcomes again. By trying to eliminate particular results, we give them energy and make them more likely to recur, similar to the self-fulfilling prophecy. What we resist, persists, because the more attention we focus on avoiding something, the more power it has over us. To live less defensively, we need to know what we want to occur in the future, rather than what we do not want to occur.

Principle Five: Attend to synchronistic events. All of us can use a little help along the way and sometimes that help is right in front of us. Since everything is connected to everything else, meaningful coincidences are actually forms of higher guidance. Our connections to the world beyond our senses form inner communications systems. Thus, we must not overlook messages from books, TV, or friends. For example, if a friend talks to me about attending a yoga class the day after I independently decide yoga would be a good idea, I should view it as a level of guidance and consider taking a yoga class now! We need to let events find us and when they do, we should not resist them. These impulses are there to help us. If we shelter ourselves from the outside world, nothing will get through and we will lose access to the most vital connection to the larger whole.

Principle Six: Anxiety signals our constraints, restrictions, and limitations. When we turn our backs on unresolved situations, we give life to their future existence. Lack of action produces the same karma we are trying to change. Thus, we should direct energy to the situations causing the most anxiety. Freud's saying, "Where id is, ego should be," can be paraphrased to, "Where anxiety is, action should be." As Kierkegaard noted, anxiety resides at the contact boundary between the old and the new. To move through the anxiety, we must take action. Since karma is action, our actions determine our fates. Knowing the action to take is easier than taking the action itself. For example, I think if I am more confident, I will overcome shyness. But to be more confident, I need to realize being shy will get in the way. In a bold act of courage, I approach someone at a party and talk to her. Through this simple, but difficult action, I become more confident and less shy. Such an uncommon act is filled with anxiety because I must advance beyond a comfort level to get to a new place.

Transcendence in Family Systems

When a person becomes aware of childhood internalizations and decides not to play by ingrained family rules, the family places enormous pressure on the person to conform. Historically, families do not like change.

Systems theory shows families maintain homeostasis by compensating in one direction for a change a family member makes in another direction. This compensatory function maintains the balance in the family. When a family member decides to break out of a habituated role, the system places equal pressure on the member to remain the same. As a result, most children exhibit differences by going to the opposite extreme. Although this polar shift produces predictable behavior patterns, it does not produce conscious identities.

The use of family pressure to have its members conform is clearly seen in exaggerated family experiences. For example, the pressure placed on an abuse victim to keep quiet is enormous, not only because of the repercussions, but because the family karma is repression. No one in a repressed family talks openly. It takes an immense act of courage to break the silence because the family member is not only breaking the cycle of abuse but also the cycle of repression. In a heroic sense, the family member is single-handedly changing the future karma of the entire family. This example illustrates how easy it is to talk about transcending family limitations and how difficult it is to take the necessary action. Similarly, when the first child from an uneducated family attends college, the historical illiteracy constraint is broken forever.

Transcendence is mystical because once we transcend the limitations of our family patterns, we can encounter opportunities beyond our childhood residue, beyond our present lifestyle, and beyond our wildest dreams.

Summary

In mysticism, everything is connected to everything else. According to major psychological theories, there are three spheres of existence: the unconscious, the conscious, and the superconscious, each being independent within the context of a larger sphere of existence. Although there are boundaries between layers, leakages occur allowing for greater awareness of the parts within the whole.

Faced with the polarity of birth and death, we question the physical and consider the metaphysical. Similar to the internalization process of the ego where one generation influences the next, karma is based on cause and effect. We are born with limiting patterns of preceding generations, along with unrestricted ability to transcend them.

Awareness is the initial intervention toward transcendence, where we reveal the false self resulting from unconscious parental identification and counter-identification. Conscious intent involves knowing we can take action, followed by taking the required action. Through conscious intent, we discover our true selves and our unique destinies.

Six principles of transcendence were presented as follows:

- Karma is not just for mystics; it is everywhere.
- Awareness is an intervention.
- Do not wait for the universe to get your attention; you will not like its methods.
- Do not live defensively.
- Attend to synchronistic events.
- Anxiety signals our constraints, restrictions, and limitations.

To transcend parental limitations is to move into a new range of being, to go where no family member has gone before, and to provide the momentum for generational progress. Transcending family limitations changes the karmic course and adds immeasurable value to the world.

Chapter Eleven: Developing A Personal Epistemology

A hidden connection is stronger than an apparent one.

Heraclitus

A s we transcend restrictive levels, the view of the world becomes less rigid. An opening occurs, in the Buddhist sense, a *satori*, where the world looks more unified. These moments of timing cannot be determined beforehand; they just happen.

While walking my daughter to preschool, I experienced such a moment and the world never looked the same again. She casually asked, "Dad, when do numbers end?" It was a natural question from a four-year-old child, but I never contemplated the numerical notion of infinite regression and progression. The notion that numbers go on forever—each number transcends the last one yet contains it in its sum total—is so simple, so basic, and yet so deep. It is space and time in action.

Happenstance and the Mathematics of Transcendence

Each number is a separate and distinct unit, yet each belongs to a class called numbers. We are individual members of a class that evolved by transcending inherited parental constraints, just as numbers evolve by transcending the previous. This fundamental act of evolution moves us forward, while contained within its movement is the prior history of space in time.

Thus, I became aware of the mystic's view of the whole contained in the part. At that moment, I realized we are the embodiment of the universe. The philosophy of the part to whole, the theological saying "as above, so below," and the creative act of awareness came together to produce this simple insight.

Before my daughter's innocent question, this flow of infinite regression and progression was as unastonishing as the fact that numbers go on forever. I never really thought about it; I accepted it as true. I never saw how numbers mirror our developmental scheme, representing human history as one generation builds on the previous one. In this scheme, I saw how Pythagoras viewed numbers as actual manifestations of universal principles.

Since my daughter's question, the knowledge I once took for granted has become part of my personal epistemology. I began to see the world differently, not based upon unconscious identifications, but through understanding and knowledge. It is uncanny how a simple question can produce such an incredible reverberation. Yet it happens all the time, even when you are just walking your daughter to preschool.

Shaping Your Personal Epistemology

Although I am not a pioneer of modern thought and everything herein has been said countless times before in more scholarly fashion, I understood these concepts by integrating them within my own experience. This is the essence of a personal epistemology—the development of a personal understanding of how the world works and each individual's place in its design.

A personal epistemology is a belief your experience tells you is true. Generally associated with philosophy, the term *epistemology* comes from the Greek *episteme*, which means knowledge. Your personal epistemology is derived from your experience of how the world is organized, and your place in that organization. Thus, the more you are aware of your personal epistemology, the more guidance you will have in overcoming personal restrictions.

A personal epistemology is dynamic, always under development. It changes, gains definition; and seeks to explain that which is just beyond our grasp.

Ultimately, the heartfelt question is: How do I know what I know is true?" Developing a personal epistemology answers this question. No matter what the intent, a worldview results from subjective analysis and personal experience assembled in an idiosyncratic way. Although we are connected in space and time, each of us perceives the connection differently. According to the subjective pragmatism of William James, "If, after the theories and imaginative work has been responsibly executed, a particular picture satisfies our temperamental requirements better than others do, then it is rational for us to have faith in it" (Myers, 1986, p.341). Taken alone, theories are limited. Only personal knowledge liberates the truth from countless theories.

Polarity Effects on Personal Epistemology

My daughter's question about numbers and The Angel from the Woods remind me that we are part of a larger web of interaction. According to the central paradox of mysticism, unity is the totality of any event grasped through an appreciation of the poles defining the whole. The law of polarity unites by bringing together opposites. It is representative of the duality of unity—out of one comes many, which in turn defines the one.

I want to share two personal experiences, one as a teenager and one as an adult, to examine how awareness of the law of polarity evolved to a personal epistemology.

Woodstock: In the summer of 1969, I was on my way to the Woodstock Music and Arts Fair with my friend Jimmy. Little did we know our pilgrimage would be a defining moment for our culture and that we were its representatives. Woodstock became our symbol of freedom and community. At a time when the anti-war sentiment was at its height, the dove and guitar symbol of Woodstock appealed to a generation of freedom-starved hippies.

Our system of government had become rigidified and could no longer address the growing demands of dissatisfied citizens who were not afraid to speak out for human rights and an end to the Vietnam War.

Rigidification produces what Kierkegaard (1849) calls *shut-upness*, or the repression of freedom. In a logical reaction to authoritarian control, our openness was triggered by the shut-upness of our predecessors. Without repression we cannot know what freedom is because we would have nothing to define it against.

Our anti-establishment sentiment hinged solely upon opposing traditional views. Like children trying to establish freedom and identity from their parents, we let it be known we were different from their generation. We did not accept war, the denigration of human rights, and the oppression of expression in any form. We voiced our disapproval by holding love-ins, be-ins, and sit-ins. We let our hair grow long and traded our ties for tie-dyes. Our arrogance was naïve because we did not understand that a true identity could never be formed in opposition. It is a human failure to consider oneself identified simply by knowing what one is not; we were anti-establishment because we had come up against the limits of the establishment and needed to break it down in order to change it.

The great Austrian author Robert Musil (1995) wrote, "Ultimately a thing exists only by virtue of its boundaries, which means by a more or less hostile act against its surroundings: without the pope there would have been no Luther, and without the pagans no pope, so there is no getting away from the fact that man's deepest social instinct is his antisocial instinct" (p. 22). By virtue of its own existence the establishment produced our anti-establishment views. We could not incorporate the old ways with the new, so we rebelled. At this point in my life the law of polarity was beginning to take form.

In the context of this extraordinary period of American history, we headed to Bethel, New York and set up camp. For two days people streamed into the surrounding fields and cow pastures of Max Yasgur's farm. We parked miles away and walked the last distance to take our place in front of the large altar that was erected for this gathering. Food ran out almost immediately and the Port O Sans were insufficient. Then the rains came. The cow pasture turned into a shit hole. Camaraderie was no longer a concept; it was the only way to live. We were loving and kind to each other and instinctively knew we shared a common bond because of the deep sense of community.

There were thousands of us, tens of thousands, and finally hundreds of thousands. As we took our seats we could see people stretched out forever. We were packed in tightly, but seemed to have all the room we needed. As we faced the altar set up at the edge of the field, it was as if we were one. It was an enormous stage with microphones and speakers so no one would miss a word of the message we came to hear. We sat in a cow pasture up to our elbows in cow shit and could not imagine it any other way. Finally, after years of planning, days of traveling, and hours of waiting, an African American man wearing a sarong came out onto the platform rhythmically playing his guitar and encouraging us to accept our freedom. This was the message we all came to hear. "Freedom. Freedom. Freedom. Freedom..." he sang. He chanted as he danced across the platform. His rhythm was hypnotic. His name was Richie Havens. Woodstock had begun.

Ayahuasca: Twenty-five years later, Marie Doren got off a plane in Peru to meet a medicine man on her vision quest in the Amazon. "We sat in cow shit the day after the ayahuasca ceremony," she explained. I was her therapist, a gray-haired survivor of the '60s with enough wisdom and balance to help people from getting lost in their own brand of magic. But when she said, "cow shit" I was back at Woodstock. Was her experience any different than mine? I listened intently, flashing back at the same time. I could feel the excitement of my old journey reawaken within me. We both ended up in cow pastures at different times and places and knew it could not have happened any other way.

"He picked us up at the airport," she explained about the medicine man. "He was wearing a T-shirt and jeans and carried an electronic Spanish/English translator. His eyes were alive like I have never seen before. He was very happy, very free. He was in his fifties and his name was Agustin Rivas." Was his presence any greater than the hypnotic rhythm of Richie Haven's freedom chant that captivated me and five hundred thousand other people?

"We flew into Iquitos, Peru and stayed in a little hotel on the edge of the water," Marie continued. "He was excited we were there and anxious to bring us back to his home." *And we have to get ourselves back to the gaaaaaarden...*Crosby, Stills, and Nash echoed in my ears. "We went downstream for three hours to his village. When we got there, we were met by ten women who carried our luggage into the jungle. It was a two-hour hike to Yushantaita, which was his home." *By the time we got to Woodstock we were half a million strong and everywhere were songs and celebrations.* "It was a total of five hours from Iquitos," Marie went on. "It looked like a scene out of *Robinson Crusoe*—the small village was set up on stilts, there were streams of pure water flowing all around the grounds, bananas adorned the trees, there were huge pots cooking in the kitchen. It was absolutely beautiful.

"On the second night our guide took us into the jungle and showed us his medicine plants. In the middle of the clearing was his altar and here he gave us our first ayahuasca drink. We had to respect it. I listened to the song *Amazing Grace* playing in my head. I wrote in my journal that I wanted to know God and to know my relationship to God. We approached him reverently and took our first ayahuasca drink."

Ayahuasca is a plant that grows judiciously throughout the Amazon and is made into a ceremonial drink used by the indigenous Amazon people for spiritual rituals. Only shamans are authorized to prepare the drink. "I was sitting on the dirt with mosquito nets over me when I was given the drink," Marie continued. "Shortly after I took it, my brain felt like it was going to split open. Some people were getting sick because the ayahuasca vine is also a purgative. I stared at the moon for grounding and stability, but got phantasmagoric images instead. I saw a woman flying out of the moon and into my left ear, and I felt my whole head start to shift, and the top of my head split open." Marie paused for a minute and then said, "I still get these sensations in my left ear and I think of the moon and the mysterious woman flying out of it and the earthy energies of the Amazon. The visions I had were really beautiful. I felt like a teenager again; something had cleansed my body and I felt like I was not separate from the earth or the heavens. I felt totally connected and in communion with everything. My eyes felt bright and alert. I felt incredible."

Marie's description of her cosmic connection is similar to the one Fritjof Capra (1975) talked about in the preface to his unifying work, *The Tao of Physics*:

> As I sat on that beach my former experiences came to life: I "saw" cascades of energy coming down from outer space, in which particles were created and destroyed in rhythmic pulses; I "saw" the atoms of the elements and those of my body participating in this cosmic dance of energy; I felt its rhythm and I "heard" its sound, and at that moment I knew that this was the Dance of Shiva, the Lord of Dancers worshiped by the Hindus.

In the Hindu tradition, when Shiva dances, the energy of the world spins into a unifying whole. Marie, Capra, and I tapped into different visions of unification through our own particular experiences and orientations. Marie took the path of the shaman, Capra took the path of the scientist, and I followed the path of my youthful exuberance. Our approaches to connecting with the whole were different, but the whole itself did not change. It has as many access points as there are people.

"Then we hiked back down to Yushantaita where bags and bags of cow shit were waiting for us upon our return," Marie continued. She went on to tell me how he placed the cow shit in the middle of a Banyan tree. "It had roots that went in a huge circle back to itself," she explained. "He piled all this cow shit right in the middle and promised we would have wealth and good luck if we did this ceremony with him. It would heal many things, he said. He started with the youngest girl, who was sixteen and had her lay down on the cow shit and then started piling more of it on top of her. She was very brave," Marie said. "We were all standing there naked in the jungle in the middle of this Banyan tree and she stood up and had it in her hair and everywhere. Then he had us hold hands and stand together and then get on the ground. We did this *ohm* together on the ground, sitting on the jungle floor naked holding hands in the middle of this Banyan tree with these people, and it was probably more powerful than anything I had ever done. It was a feeling of total connection and feeling very earthy with shit all over you—just very connected as we made a human circle within the circle of the Banyan roots."

Marie finished her story by saying, "This connection to a higher self, an inner sense of belonging, is one I still remember strong in my bones. I feel that way now with my family, but I will always carry the experience of feeling it on a higher plane where identity fuses with belonging and does not sacrifice one part to the other."

I was reminded of my Woodstock experience where we shared three days of what Max Yasgur called, "peace and love, and nothing but peace and love." The peaceful coexistence at Woodstock was symbolized by the peace sign we flashed to one another, a simple gesture of shared meaning and connection. But this sense of connection I felt with Marie went deeper than the incredible hallucinogenic experience we shared. The polarity of cow shit and consciousness held us together. For both of us, the experience of a mystical state in the context of manure was our entry into mysticism.

Through my experience at Woodstock and working with many people like Marie who have had simultaneous experiences of the mystical and the mundane, I have learned that polarities represent wholeness. Consequently, personal and relationship growth is dependent upon integrating the polarities in our lives. My personal epistemology was advanced by my continuing study of the mystical and the mundane.

Integrating the Mystical and the Mundane

In the personal crusade toward higher consciousness two things are certain: (1) no matter how advanced we think we are, we are still lower animal forms that have bodily functions, and; (2) since human beings are higher animal forms containing consciousness, we become self-conscious of our own physicality. Recognizing the enormous role polarities play in human development, Ernest Becker (1973) wrote a beautiful passage about the human response to being physical in *The Denial of Death*. I quote its entirety:

> Excreting is the curse that threatens madness because it shows man his abject finitude, his physicalness, the likely unreality of his hopes and dreams. But even more immediately, it represents man's utter bafflement at the sheer *non-sense* of creation: to fashion the sublime miracle of the human face, the *mysterium tremendum* of radiant feminine beauty, the veritable goddesses that beautiful women are; to bring this out of nothing, out of the void, and make it shine in noonday; to take such a miracle and put miracles again within it, deep in the mystery of eyes that peer out—the eyes that gave even dry Darwin a chill: to do all this, and to combine it with an anus that shits! It is too much. Nature mocks us, and poets live in torture (p. 33-34).

Becker stuns us with his prose and exhorts us to accept physicality as a matter of fact. His blunt assessment of the human condition signals the "tremendous mystery" in the connection between the polarities of beauty and the anus. He refers to the *mysterium tremendeum*, the polarities of the mystical and the mundane, inextricably woven deep into the soul of people.

On a larger scale, the dichotomy of cow shit and consciousness reflects this part to whole relationship. Cow shit represents the earth and everything mundane, while consciousness represents the larger context of the mystical. Together they form one complete gestalt uniting the mystical and the mundane to produce a profound insight about the order of the universe. When Marie and I were immersed in cow shit, there was no self-consciousness, just the divine sense of connection between two distinct realms.

Heraclitus tried to bring the understanding of the mysterium tremendeum to his students by teaching them the world was connected through opposing forces, both seen and unseen, mystical and mundane, that together create a hidden harmony in the universe.

In fragment 9 Heraclitus spoke of paired opposites forming a unified whole by saying; "We have as One in us that which is living and dead, waking and sleeping, young and old." In an ironic twist of fate, Heraclitus died suffering from dropsy, a disease he tried to cure by immersing himself in a cowshed hoping that the warmth of the manure would draw the infection from his body (Geldard, 2000). In the end, the old Greek sage and spiritual leader, who brought light to the mystery of life, spent his last days soaking in cow shit. How befitting that his life reached its ultimate conclusion with his body awash in manure and his spirit soaring toward the heavens.

My personal epistemology is based on the law of polarity. It takes an extraordinary event, like Woodstock, to see how one level of reality intersects with a completely different level of reality, connecting them both. That is the nature of the law of polarity. Two things exist simultaneously, on opposite poles and together they produce one unified whole. It is a remarkable thing to behold, as Becker showed us, and even more remarkable to think that in our everyday lives there are always two poles defining every experience.

Summary

As we transcend previous restrictive levels, the view of the world becomes less rigid. Seemingly random events help us see the world as a more unified whole. Chance occurrences, innocent questions, and unexpected encounters are not random. A personal understanding of how the world works and each individual's place in it marks the beginning of a personal epistemology. My personal epistemology explains how:

- The law of polarity brings together opposites and represents the duality of unity—out of one comes many, which in turn defines the one.

- Polarities need to be identified and polar positions modified, for a person to experience balance.
- Reality is an intermingling of subjective experience superimposed on external conditions.
- In the striving for higher consciousness, we cannot transcend physicality, but we can overcome self-consciousness about it.
- Personal knowledge liberates us from countless theories.

A personal epistemology is dynamic, keeps us constantly striving, and ultimately brings us closer to transcendence. Recognizing patterns is the first step toward changing them. A personal epistemology helps determine the direction of change. As we progress, we overcome restrictions and enact moments of transcendence. The more moments of transcendence we experience, the more our lives move forward with meaning and purpose.

Chapter Twelve: Becoming Conscious

> *You would not find out the boundaries of the soul, even by traveling along every path, so deep a measure does it have.*
>
> Heraclitus

Throughout this book, we have seen how the law of polarity affects individuals, couples, and families. But it goes beyond, even impacting global politics. Since the upsurge of terrorist attacks, patriotism has lead to unity born of terrorism, dividing the world using the poles of good and evil. This oft-used leitmotif is a clear-cut example of racism and hatred prevalent throughout history.

Although world integration may be slow in coming, personal integration does not have to wait. The development of an authentic self is the first step to integrating polarities. Then we must proceed to integrate ourselves into a splintered world.

The Conscious Self

Building a conscious self requires the exploration into a unique structure—the true *I* in *I am*. It is not the embodiment or rejection of parental personalities, but the conscious spirit in each of us.

In the conscious self, experiences are organized so they are under control, instead of mere unconscious internalizations. In Winnicott's terms, the false self developed in childhood as a reaction against environmental influences builds a defensive personality. The false self naturally hides and protects the true self from environmental effects, such as hatred and rejection. The false self shields from outside dangers, thus denying the existence of the true self in favor of its own false identity. To build the conscious self, we must be aware of the true/false split.

Synthesizing the conscious and the unconscious: Jung was dynamic in the area of polarity integration. He noted that an imbalance in a person's conscious life will eventually lead to a compensatory action in his or her unconscious life. In his most notable contributions to polarity and compensation theories, he developed the psychological types of anima/animus, introvert/extrovert, and persona/shadow. These opposites constitute an entire spectrum of behavior. Since one pole cannot be separated from the other, the more we deny one side of ourselves, the more that side seeks expression through unconscious activities. Jung (1971) was clear in his assertion that:

> Every process that goes too far immediately and inevitably calls forth compensations, and without these there would be neither a normal metabolism nor a normal psyche. In this sense we can take the theory of compensation as a basic law of psychic behavior. Too little on one side results in too much on the other. Similarly, the relation between conscious and unconscious is compensatory (p. 330).

Compensation theory suggests that the pole that we ignore, disown, or project always comes back to challenge us. The more completely we identify with one pole, the stronger the projection or the denial of the opposite pole. For instance, if we deny our aggressive impulses so as not to be confrontational, we will either attract confrontational people or agitating situations wherein we can no longer avoid confrontation. If we are invested in showing the world how good we are, we experience unconscious balances through negative characteristics such as forgetfulness, rebelliousness, or gossip, thus undermining the goodness.

To have a balanced personality the conscious and unconscious parts of a person must be integrated. It is not desirable to hold the ideal that consciousness must overcome unconscious motivations—both are necessary for balance. The unconscious protects us from being overwhelmed by stimuli we cannot process. Although repression of information can lead to destructive tendencies, we never lose access to the unconscious. It is always available to us. Just as transcendence must not eliminate the need for physical and emotional experiences, the integration of conscious and unconscious aspects of ourselves must not eliminate the unconscious function. We need to access the unconscious to remove restrictions interfering with our desired functioning.

Getting serious: The first step in building a conscious self is to address polar imbalances. If we move away from problems, the problems will find us. Thus, we must make solving those problems the most serious tasks of our lives. Consider patterns such as being late, not having time for ourselves, dealing with negative relationships, being dominated by unfinished business with parents, children, or mates. When we elevate these to the realm of important issues, we make a commitment to take our karma seriously. These repetitive themes play like bad background music, becoming so familiar we forget they represent problems we need to solve.

The development of a conscious self is an intentional process, not created by default. It must be viewed seriously for us to move past habituated behaviors. If we have a situation, such as a parent we cannot reason with, a child out of control, or a relationship not functioning properly, now is the time to do something about it. Otherwise, we will never move forward in those areas. If we have unresolved issues with people who are no longer alive, or with people who are inaccessible, we may need to learn to let go, to forgive, or to gain more understanding in order for us to move forward. Creating a conscious self requires we resolve energy-draining issues so we can redistribute our resources to more worthy places.

A Guide to Becoming Conscious

In the *Macrosystemic Model of Psychotherapy* (1997), I maintained that it takes an autonomous action to change a system. We cannot control our family members or partners—only ourselves. Individually, we must make efforts to become more conscious.

Although many exercises described in Chapters Eight and Nine are geared to couples, they are equally applicable to individuals. For example, a couple's redundant loop style cannot be changed until the individual patterns of communication are changed.

The following six-question guide is a means for getting beyond personal constraints and becoming conscious. The guide is consistent with the six principles of transcendence and has direct application. It will help increase awareness of patterns, choices, and unique abilities, resulting in the synthesis of unconscious needs with conscious motivations.

1) What are my patterns? Behavior patterns have continuity from day one to the present time. Thus, we can evaluate childhood effects on current situations by understanding the repetitive nature of these patterns. First, we must recognize that problems, issues, or themes do not go away. By analyzing past behaviors we can determine patterns. Are we angry? Irritable? Self-sacrificing? Gullible? Overly emotional? Do we have a hard time setting goals? Keeping to a structure? Disciplining ourselves?

A pattern may remit for a while, but maintains a presence throughout life. By observing patterns, we can see our karma or the effects of our actions. To identify personal karma, ask this question: What do I do that leads to negative consequences? Since we cause the good and bad in our lives, we must identify the results of our actions. Then we can see the effects we so readily blame on others. For instance, if we are always in loveless relationships, we should ask what we do to create lack of love. Do we push people away? Are we cold? Are we critical? Are we afraid? By honestly looking at our actions, we can see behavioral patterns tracing back to childhood, or to family karma. Were our parents cold or aloof? Did they treat us with respect and encouragement or were they critical? Looking at how our parents behaved, we realize we behave in the same or opposite manner. For every domain and situation we can ask: What do I do that leads to negative consequences?

2) Who do I attract? Why do I attract certain people? The attraction force is compelling because it unites people operating at the same emotional level. We attract people who are both like and unlike our internal patterning. By dealing with them, rather than blaming them, we have the opportunity to grow and become more whole. If we acknowledge personal responsibility in choosing bosses, parents, and mates, we see the benefit of dealing with them rather than feeling victimized or outraged.

By examining the people in our lives, we learn about ourselves. For example, overreacting to a domineering boss indicates a wish to be domineering or a problem being subservient. Overreacting to a defensive spouse shows personal defensiveness or a pattern of putting people on the defensive.

To change the kind of people we attract, we need to change our underlying patterns. Since patterns produce outcomes, if we change our patterns, we also change our outcomes.

3) How was my identity formed? To answer this question, we must scrutinize the aspects of our parents we have incorporated and rejected. In fragment 49 Heraclitus warns, "We should not act like children of our parents." By acting like our parents, we have not progressed beyond them; we have not transcended them. To determine if behavior is consistent with intent, ask the question: *How do I want to act?* By identifying how we want to act, we base future behavior patterns on personal principles instead of childhood internalizations.

4) How am I connected mentally, physically, and spiritually? We study the interconnections between the three major levels of our existence—the mental, physical, and spiritual—to understand how these levels support each other. Since each level is connected to the other, operating at one level affects the other levels. Consider a person who excels at work, but has terrible personal relationships. At work she has a take-charge attitude and puts vision and energy into new projects. At home she expects to be taken care of and has little energy or vision for new relationship experiences. Although natural polarities, these show two distinct styles, one successful and one unsuccessful. The cure is simple, but not easy. She needs to learn to treat her personal life like her business life. Likewise, we may be successful in physical, mental, or spiritual practices, but rarely in all three. To become more balanced, we must take behaviors in the most successful area and apply them to the other areas.

5) What are my strengths, talents, and natural abilities? We live in a world focused on wrongs and weaknesses rather than strengths. It is a deficit model world replete with labels. The persistent use of positive affirmations shows we are on the opposite pole of strength, trying to condition ourselves to think positively. Systems, such as medical care, insurance coverage, mental health services, and the courts focus on wrongs rather than taking preventative measures.

Yet we all have strengths, unique talents, or natural abilities that make life easier and more enjoyable. While some people have obvious musical talents and athletic abilities, most of us must rely on subtle clues to locate our hidden abilities. We may be good organizers, problem-solvers, decision-makers, or facile with written or spoken words. We may have green thumbs, good judgment, keen insight, exceptional eye-hand coordination, fortitude, will power, or spatial acuity. The list is infinite. Unfortunately, we often take our natural abilities for granted since we did not have to put much energy into developing them. To become conscious, we must become aware of what is natural for us and then learn to exploit those qualities for the rest of our lives.

6) What do I expect of myself? After examining the previous five questions, we ask about our expectations. What are our dreams and ambitions? How do we expect to achieve them? The answer to these questions serves as a guide to the future self, the one lacking full definition, but under conscious control. Our imaginations are limitless and so are possible attainments. Many people in the public eye have risen from obscurity to unimaginable positions of power, wealth, and fame. Their credo is: If you can dream it, you can achieve it. Our imaginings, thoughts, and dreams—personal and individual identifiers—indicate what we expect from ourselves and what we want from life. By imagining the future, we gain direction and learn what we have to do to fulfill our destinies.

In his classic book *Man's Search for Meaning*, Victor Frankl (1959) beautifully and simply illustrated that life without meaning and direction is life without purpose. "Everyone has his own specific vocation or mission in life," he writes, "to carry out a concrete assignment which demands fulfillment. Therein he cannot be replaced, nor can his life be repeated. Thus, everyone's task is as unique as is his specific opportunity to implement it" (p. 113). Rather than ask what we expect of life, Frankl asks, "What does life ask of us?" Whether we approach the meaning of life from one pole or the other, when we find answers to our problems and take actions to accomplish future dreams, we fulfill life's request.

Kierkegaard purported that a human being is a synthesis, a containment of both body and soul, of finite and infinite, of freedom and restriction. To become more whole, we must take these opposite characteristics and integrate them into a seamless personality structure. As we find the answers to problems, constraints contract, leaving more energy to pursue the future.

But the act of change is anything but easy. Even with a foundation of understanding, it takes vigilance, determination, a sense of will, and practice to break patterns.

Once grasped, patterns can unexpectedly reemerge. In my practice, I see people for six to eight successive sessions to get an understanding of their particular issues. During that time, they build momentum, gain direction, develop intention, and their lives begin to change. Our meetings taper off as they ride the momentum of early success.

As any boxcar driver knows, momentum grinds to a halt when the natural laws of gravity take over. To keep momentum going, we cannot stop pushing. When we do, the old patterns reestablish themselves and feelings of failure set in. We assume if we work on building strength and direction, momentum will follow. On the contrary, we build strength and direction by moving into action. If we make ourselves move, the rest will follow. If we wait to be moved, we may wait a long time. In the end, conscious intention requires discipline and action.

Identification Through Negation

Although I advocate an insightful, thought process in creating a conscious self, it is not the only approach. Those not inclined to use insight-oriented therapies can become conscious without probing the depths of the unconscious mind. Since the law of polarity requires two aspects of the same issue, we can become more complete by identifying what we are not.

Negation, identifying what we are not, results in defining what we are. This ancient type of apophatic reasoning has been used to elevate people to high levels of personal integrity.

To begin the process, identify the qualities you do not want to represent your character and the related behaviors. For example, if you do not want to be cold and aloof, list the behaviors signaling coldness and aloofness, such as being withdrawn, unfriendly and disinterested. Then make sure you are not representing them in your character. By keeping this list in mind, you will become more receptive, more talkative, and ask questions to convey interest in other people.

Since we choose to move away from that which we dislike, the process of negation can develop a conscious self. But be careful not to move completely to the opposite pole. For instance, if you do not want to be distant, you may become intrusive if you exhibit the opposite behavior. Rather than lose the boundary altogether, be curious or more questioning instead. The goal is to create balance rather than react by adopting the opposite behaviors. We do not want to tempt the fate that befell Icarus when he strayed too far from the middle course. The idea of identification by negation is to establish balance, not extremes.

Self-integration: In the part-to-whole philosophy, the hierarchy is built on self-sustaining, independent parts, that are dependent on larger wholes to fulfill their greater purpose. Wilber (1995) takes this notion one step further, purporting that each successive level transcends, yet includes the previous level. Through the process of inclusion, each successive level grows beyond the previous level, but contains the marker of the previous level. Similarly, in our numerical system, each number contains and transcends the previous number. For instance, the number two contains the number one within it, but transcends the number one because its sum is greater.

As we integrate and transcend we grow, but only if the restrictions of the previous level are resolved in the new structure. The previous level of organization must be incorporated so it extends the next level of functioning, rather than provide the same degree of restriction in a more complex form.

Maslow's (1968) hierarchy of needs, from basic physical requirements to self-actualization is a perfect example. Self-integration occurs through the inclusion and transcendence of previous levels of personality development. At the level of self-actualization, we are free to determine the future without perpetuating previous patterns, since they have been resolved.

The more resolution we have to previous events in our lives, the more the world opens up to us in unimaginable ways. From interviews with many self-actualized people, Maslow discovered they continued to have peak experiences of intense insight providing a sense of freedom from ego restraints and defensiveness. They came closer to the egoless state of peace and union characteristic of the mystical experience.

By integrating the self and becoming more conscious, we move up the hierarchy of needs to an emotionally-grounded level, where we can incorporate the mystical into our lives. Otherwise, mystical experiences of union become a glamorized endpoint. Like all glamorizations, the more we focus on them, the less capable we are of achieving them. With meaning and purpose, we elevate ourselves to levels of consciousness beyond description, but within reach. From these heights, we can see the polarities of man's inhumanity to man as well as the limitless potential for goodness and grace. We can better understand why May, Maslow, Rogers, and other founders of the humanistic movement chose the name *humanistic psychology* for their calling.

Emotional objectivity results in a heightened sense of awareness where the world appears as an infinite mixture of potential, possibilities, and promise. William Blake (1982), the foremost mystical poet of his time, captured this concept in his poem *The Marriage of Heaven and Hell*. He wrote, "If the doors of perception were cleansed, everything would appear to man as it is: infinite."

Pioneering the True Self

The call: Winnicott observed how the child presents a false self to the world based on his reactions to environmental impingements. The true self, or what he called the core self, remains buried beneath the reactions and counter reactions the child develops to the world around him. This is similar to Plato's "Meno" (1963a) wherein he purported that the interior wisdom we possess contains our unique identities and connects us to the wider universe. Within our unique structures, we have a calling, what Plato (1963b) refers to as the *Daemon*. A splintered and spiritual facet, it whispers to us in early life and remains like an itch upon the soul until we pay attention to it. Winnicott's true self and Plato's Daemon are one and the same. Although Plato ascribed fate to the Daemon, fate resides within the true self as a unique outcome. Through the expression of uniqueness, we define ourselves as being different from others.

By being authentic, we pass on true, new, and original aspects. They are bona fide facets of ourselves not replicable and manifested only through personal intention. According to Heschel (1965), "The authentic individual is neither an end nor a beginning, but a link between ages, both memory and expectation. Every moment is a new beginning within a continuum of history. Humbly, the past defers to the future, but it refuses to be discarded. Only he who is an heir is qualified to be a pioneer" (p. 99).

We are the heirs of life and, as true pioneers, must possess our uniquenesses. Otherwise, if we discard our passions and rationalize our actions, we deprive ourselves of our rightful heritages. By freeing the true self from its false imprisonment, each of us can break the spell of early personality influence. We can reposition ourselves for conscious, future growth.

Answering the call: The development of the true self is the end result of becoming conscious. But the true self does not move us to future callings. Rather it develops a personality free from constraints and lends support to pursue the calling.

A less constrained personality is more conflict free, leaving more energy to do other things. The question becomes: What do we want to do with our conflict-free time?

We answer this question by considering things we have wanted to experience. It can be anything; big or small, keeping in mind the small things are just as significant as the big ones. Since everything is connected to everything else, we have access to the greater whole through the smaller parts. Some people have the desire to travel but never do; others want to take music lessons, but it is never the right time; while others are interested in spending more time with particular people, but never make the proper arrangements. Conflict-free time can be used to do anything.

The six questions earlier in this chapter help determine patterns, restrictions, strengths, and expectations. The final step is to move beyond constraints, to an inventive application of the true self through action.

In other words, do something! Do not be fooled into thinking the only true callings are ones dealing with large issues, such as global peace or world hunger.

The personal calling is unique to each of us and has immense value in the world. For instance, one client used his conflict-free time to begin a coin collection, a dream since childhood. Through coin collecting, he became interested in the minting system and took his family, including his grandson, to Washington DC to visit the US mint. Enamored with the Washington area, the grandson decided to work there after college. Through his subsequent work in Washington, his contribution to society was much greater than his grandfather's coin collection. But he never forgot the origins of his professional life. As one thing is connected to another, a small action, such as collecting coins, can produce a big result over time.

In the search for authenticity, we must study the true pioneers of life. They are the original thinkers and doers who display elements of the true self we can model. A true pioneer hears his particular call and, in answering it, is brought into the underlying depth of the universe.

Winnicott was one such pioneer. He did not put energy into converting others to his point of view or assume a theoretical perspective because others accepted it. Instead, he invested his energy in representing his views as consistent with his belief system. He did not sacrifice his true self for a false sense of belonging to an elite club of analysts. Winnicott (1990) was unfailing in his devotion to the notion of the true self. He writes convincingly:

> Poets, philosophers, and seers have always concerned themselves with the idea of a true self and the betrayal of the self has been unacceptable. Shakespeare, perhaps to avoid being smug, gathered a bundle of truths to be presented by a crashing bore called Polonius. In this way we can take the advice:
>
> This above all: to thine own self be true,
> And it must follow, as the night the day,
> Thou canst not then be false to any man (p. 65-66).

Nothing is insignificant. The calling is unique to each of us and we should invest in it as if our lives depended on it. It moves us and if we are sufficiently moved, we will move others through our actions.

Summary

This chapter focused on methods for progressing to the true self. Getting in touch with the true self requires eliminating habituated childhood behaviors. In a conscious self, behaviors are under control rather than emanating from unconscious internalizations. To build the conscious self, we first must become aware of the true/false split used to self protect, since it leads to imbalances and compensatory actions in the unconscious. We then proceed to actively address unresolved issues and remove restrictions to achieve a balanced and integrated state of consciousness.

To develop a conscious self, we need to:

- Become aware of our polar imbalances.
- Identify the patterns that these imbalances indicate require integration.
- Realize how we contribute to the patterns.
- Understand how the patterns were established.
- Make the patterns the most serious things in our lives.
- Determine the natural strengths, abilities, and talents at our disposal.
- Move beyond our constraints by integrating the polar imbalances limiting us.

Negation is another means of revealing the true self. By identifying what we are not, we are defining what we are. In listing qualities unlike ourselves, we should make sure our behaviors are consistent and not opposite reactions.

Getting to the true self requires self-integration, wherein restrictions of the previous level are resolved in a new structure, opening the world in unimaginable ways. We advance to an emotionally-grounded level where we can incorporate the mystical. The development of the true self results in a more conflict-free life, leaving energy to act on the unique and important calling within each of us.

Chapter Thirteen: Conclusion

If we do not expect the unexpected
we will not discover it.

Heraclitus

As we have seen, human personality is a blend of opposites, a synthesis. Humans have a finite existence within the infinite history of the universe.

By examining unconscious development from early childhood, we determine our likes and dislikes. As a result, we feel more unique and separate, while at the same time becoming more genuinely connected to others. In establishing separateness and connection through conscious intent, we use the law of polarity for synthesis rather than split the world to self-protect, as in early identification.

Polarities create the great divide of the psyche. We see the effects in every aspect of life and in the contradictory nature of the universe. One part is connected to a higher calling, what Plato calls *the immortal soul*, and the other part is earth-bound.

The higher calling involves self-reflection and questioning such as: Who am I? Where did I come from? Where am I going?

The earth-bound aspect is mechanical and deals with everyday life tasks. Both parts are essential to the human experience and cannot be separated. A higher consciousness is as important as sitting in the mud.

Unity and Duality

The fundamental contradiction of polarities begins with the realization that the source of nurturing and frustration comes from the same person, mother. Being too young to deal with the contradiction that one person is the source of both good and bad feelings, infants split those effects. This is a natural split since the universe is fractured and based upon polarities for its existence.

As Heraclitus taught, without polar points we can never appreciate, or even contemplate, the whole. The infant's merger and split with mother is the first journey into the fractured world and is a logical repetition of the macro pattern. In adulthood, we heal the split and become more complete, more whole, and more in touch with the unity to which we will one day return.

During the journey on earth, good and bad impulses are contained internally and projected externally, creating the biggest life challenge—to integrate contradictory feelings, emotions, and experiences into one coherent personality.

The Process of Integration

In terms of ego psychology, Mahler termed the coming together of disparate maternal parts in the child's psyche as *rapprochement*, a reunification of the mother and the child after separation. Once a child has split the world into opposing parts, he comes to understand that mother is neither good nor bad, but both, and returns to her with less conflict and anxiety. Repeatedly, this becomes the task throughout life, the integration of good and bad experiences into one coherent and conscious pattern.

A person abused by a parent as a child must learn to deal with contradictory emotions of loving and hating the abuser and integrate a personality style that does not perpetuate the abuse. On the other hand, he must not deny his aggressive tendencies and act as if anger is a detached emotion having no place in his life.

For the divorced person, the next relationship must be a conscious choice resulting from an awareness of the bad aspects of the first relationship, without denying it for its opposite manifestation. Otherwise, the next choice will not be better, as in the case of poor Toni Buddenbrook.

The process of integration happens, like it or not and with or without awareness. As we replicate situations, we become more frustrated and unhappy, until we are forced to change or give into the mechanical laws of survival of the fittest. We cannot escape life's lessons because life is the greatest teacher. Life forces each of us to determine a path, choose a major in college, choose a mate, and then resolve the contradictions inherent in all of these choices.

As a young man I wanted to have a private practice where I could be my own boss, set my own schedule, and do the work I really loved. Ten years after meeting those goals, I was dealing with the reality. I had no health benefits, paid vacations, or sick leave, no predictable paycheck, and no break from the demand of being available to the people who counted on me. What happened to the freedom of setting my own schedule and being my own boss? I was forced to deal with the contradictions of my dream and to find a middle ground. In short, I had to resolve the polarities created when I decided to be my own boss. My desire for freedom contained inherent limitations only integrated through the acceptance of both polarities.

Parts and Wholes

If there were more personal and global integration there would be less division. But we routinely encounter the act of separating or splitting into parts. Since the universe must be divided to be whole, we are faced with life's greatest contradiction—being an individual who is part of a collective.

As part of the larger whole, we inherit fragmented worldviews from the primordial split in the universe. The element of splitting, followed closely by the mechanism of projection, works deep into the personality during childhood and remains within, seeking resolution at every life stage.

Just as the universe comes into existence the moment it perceives itself, Hofstadter (1979) says, "The self comes into being the moment it has the power to reflect itself" (p. 709). As we become conscious, we produce our own versions of reality by drawing distinctions based on polar positions. First we identify or counter-identify with our parents. Then we use the law of polarity to make distinctions between right and wrong, good and bad, morality and immorality, love and hate, and so on, until we have a sense of self.

At this point of development, we think we know where we are coming from. But we fail to recognize that our personal points of view reflect the initial split in the universe by being only partially correct. As Wilber (1977) says in his groundbreaking book the *Spectrum of Consciousness*, "when the universe is severed into a subject vs. an object, into one state which sees vs. one state which is seen, *something always gets left out*. In this condition, the universe will always partially elude itself" (p. 36-37).

Self-reflection allows us to know we are both subject and object simultaneously and that there are two sides to every story. Our views of other people, including our parents, spouses, and children are hindered by the inability to see the whole picture.

As we mature, we appreciate that we see only part of the truth. Although true in its own right, it is not the whole truth. We learn we can never see people for who they really are because of the fragmentation of a singular vision, what Bateson called monocular vision. By trying to discern right from wrong, we engage in lengthy discourse, expressing our particular views. Thus, language is the essential means of communication.

The Limitations of Language

As a symbol of human advancement, language is quite restrictive. In the Buddhist tradition, language keeps us from experiencing the world beyond the senses. It acts as a distorting filter, taking pure energy and transforming it into intellectual thoughts. By going beyond language, the ego, and the duality of subject/object, we can merge with pure consciousness.

Practices such as mindfulness, self-attention, and silence are tools designed to shut down inner chatter and expand consciousness into the realm of the mystical. But these higher states of consciousness are impractical in the Western world. We are always learning, looking for the next growth experience, and tackling point A so we can get to point B.

In the *Tractatus* (1961), Wittgenstein acknowledges a world outside of the one accessible by human perception, but does not try to unite these two realities. They must remain separate because the logic of the human thought process hinges upon language. It becomes a barrier between our experiences of the world and what may lie beyond.

Consistent with the Buddhist philosophy, Wittgenstein maintains we are not located within language. The true self is reachable only beyond language. At the highest level of enlightenment, we can briefly step outside of language; but we cannot live outside of language. The task is to learn to be mindful without disengaging from the world in the pursuit of mindfulness.

The True Self

As mentioned in the introductory chapter, we do not want to lose ourselves in the pursuit of mindfulness, transcendence or enlightenment. Merging with the singular source results in the loss of humanity. The task is to identify the true self by being separate and distinct within a unified field of consciousness. Through self-reflection, we realize we are separate and connected simultaneously. We learn to keep individuality while merging to form larger wholes, such as marriages, communities, states, and global economies.

The greatest self-reflection occurs in pondering the question: Who am I? By focusing on the *I* in *I am*, we descend into the unique qualities of a single point within the unified field. To answer the question, *Who am I,* we must first understand where we come from, how the world works, and why we act as we do. The purpose of this book was to provide the framework to explore these questions.

Since we organize ourselves in the same way the universe organizes itself, we can see the law of polarity affecting every aspect of our lives. By now, the reader can appreciate how the law of polarity influences both large and small actions, from magnetic forces, to identity formation, and to theological, philosophical, and religious practices.

In accordance with the central paradox of mysticism, everything governing the world outside of ourselves is also within us, giving direct knowledge of the universe through self-exploration. The macrocosm feeds the microcosm, which in turn reflects the whole in its smallest manifestation. Thus, we encounter the whole by studying any one of its parts. In other words, the more we study ourselves, the more we encounter the mysteries and paradoxes of the universe.

Although we live in an interconnected universe, we each have special talents, beliefs, and a singular calling. We each feel a call to do something unique. In the back of our minds, we hear the whispers telling us when to change jobs, move to different cities, or pick up books containing one sentence out of ten thousand, written just for us. In these moments, we know there is some force greater than ourselves, an intelligence we can tap into, but cannot see. To tap into this potential, we need to listen to the call. Sometimes by just listening, our lives change. It can be so simple and so deep.

The task is to reach a level where the true self comes from a conscious place. From that point on, we find integrity by being true to our selves. The true self is conscious and awake, not an unconscious abstraction of a distant internalization. We are not denying our early internalizations. Karma is dependent on it. But we are not meant to work and rework karma for an entire lifetime. We are meant to grow beyond childhood karma and place our unique fingerprints on the future.

As we saw with the Angel from the Woods, in moments of life and death we can see synchronicity in its ever-present forms and we know beyond a doubt there is more to life than meets the eye. At these times, we are connected to something far greater than we can see and we know life is a meaningful representation of this larger picture.

Usually, we feel small and insignificant at times of immense awe. But realizing the connection between the macrocosm and the microcosm, between the part and the whole, we can rest assured that whatever our contributions, they will reverberate throughout the universe. Small changes can go unnoticed, but over time these fluctuations become quite dramatic. Meteorologist Edward Lorenz (1994) made a case for these generative changes by observing that a butterfly fluttering its wings in Japan could cause a gale-force wind in North America. What seems small today, such as the promise to save one dollar a day in an interest bearing account, will have tremendous implications twenty years from now.

With the law of polarity as mysticism's representative, we are humbled by the physical separation from the mystical state and seek union through spirituality, religion, meditation, and other forms of higher consciousness training. It pushes us to reach, to achieve, to strive, and to search.

For the young adult going out into the world the saying, "You can never go home again." is true enough. But in life, we constantly try to find peace by returning to the unity from which we came.

Acknowledgments

My mom and dad have always been my inspiration. They understood their heritage and sought a better life for themselves and their children. They encouraged me each step of the way and gave me every reason to believe in myself.

In addition, this book would not be possible without my association with Gregge Tiffen. I learned significant metaphysical concepts and principles from Gregge long before I read them in any textbook. Gregge's work is incomparable.

I was introduced to Gregge by my first mentor, Barbra Dillenger, who continues to unveil the extraordinary in the ordinary, even in the most mundane situations.

To my wife, Joyce, for her enduring love and support.

To my children, Caryn and Evan, who remind me every day how the mystical and the mundane work together to produce rare and wonderful results.

To my brother, David, who has always been one step ahead of me. I might not have earned a master's degree in social work if he had not thought of it first. And to my sister, Evie, who gave our family the right balance and experience with diversity.

To my good friends Lois Tema and Bonnie Beck for their careful reading and considerate editing of early drafts of the book.

To John Borck for pushing my range of thinking with his creative brilliance and insight.

To my extended family at Harmonium, Inc. where I have been the Chief Clinical Director for more than twenty-six years. This community-based agency is a living example of the part-to-whole philosophy of mysticism. By carving out its own identity within the community, Harmonium has added strength to both the part and the whole. In particular, I want to mention former Executive Director Nancy Sherman for her vision and command, Rob Cureton, Ph.D., for his creative brilliance, Michelle Zeidler, MSW, for her tenacity and diligence, Tracy Wutzke, Ph.D., for tying it all together with grace and charm, and Bill Grove, MFT, for his firm and unwavering commitment throughout the years.

I am grateful to all of my clients, some of whom read early manuscript drafts to ensure the concepts held true to my work. They have been an endless source of inspiration and have given me the privilege of learning about life by entrusting me with theirs.

To my editor, Patricia Benesh, whose vision brought coherence, continuity, and structure to the book.

To Angela Hoy for seamlessly bringing the book to press.

To Doris Doi for her refinements throughout the book.

My heartfelt appreciation goes to my gifted friend Lois Sunrich for her outstanding publication assistance.

And finally, to Joel Singer, Paul Harnick, Bob Green, Andrew Sussman, and Mel Jankolovits, lifelong New York friends who continue to help me develop ideas of connection even though I have created a separate life in California.

References

Bateson, G., Jackson, D. D., Haley, J., & Weakland, J. H. (1956).
Toward a theory of schizophrenia. *Behavioral Science, 1,* 251-264.

Bateson, G. (1972). *Steps to an Ecology of Mind.* New Jersey: Jason
Aronson, Inc.

Bateson, G. (1979). *Mind and Nature: A necessary unity.* New York:
Dutton.

Bateson, M. C. (1984). *Peripheral Visions: Learning along the way.*
New York: Harper Collins.

Becker, E. (1962). *The Birth and Death of Meaning: An interdisciplinary
perspective on the problem of man.* New York: The Free Press.

Becker, E. (1973). *The Denial of Death.* New York: The Free Press.

Bertalanffy, L., von. (1968). *General System Theory.* New York: George
Braziller.

Blake, W. (1982). The Marriage of Heaven and Hell. *The Complete
Poetry and Prose of William Blake.* New York: Anchor Books.

Bohr, N. (1958). *Atomic Physics and Human Knowledge.* NY: John
Wiley & Sons.

Borges, J. L., (1999). Blindness. *Jorge Luis Borges: Selected non-
fictions.* New York: Viking Press.

Bowen, M. (1978). *Family Therapy in Clinical Practice.* New York:
Jason Aronson, Inc.

Canetti, E. (1999). *The Memoirs of Elias Canetti.* New York: Farrar,
Straus & Giroux.

Capra, F. (1975). *The Tao of Physics.* Boulder, CO: Shambhala
Publications.

Doi, T. (1973). *The Anatomy of Dependence,* translated J. Bester. Japan:
Kodansha International Press.

Eddington, A. S. (1923). *Mathematical Theory of Relativity.* Cambridge,
MA: Cambridge University Press.

Emerson, R. W. (1979). *The Essays of Ralph Waldo Emerson.*
Cambridge, MA: The Belknap Press.

Frankl, V. (1959). *Man's Search for Meaning: An introduction to
logotherapy.* New York: Simon & Schuster.

Freud, S. (1900). *The Interpretation of Dreams.* Standard Edition, Vol.
4&5, London: Hogarth, 1955.

Freud, S. (1920). *Beyond the Pleasure Principle.* Standard Edition, Vol. 18, London: Hogarth,1955.

Freud, S. (1926). *Inhibitions, Symptoms, and Anxiety.* Standard Edition, Vol. 20. London: Hogarth Press, 1959.

Freud, S. (1965). *The New Introductory Lectures on Psychoanalysis.* New York: W. W. Norton & Company.

Frost, R. (1995). *Frost: Collected poems, prose, & plays.* US: The Library of America.

Geldard, R. (2000). *Remembering Heraclitus.* US: Lindisfarne Books.

Gergen, K. (1991). *The Saturated Self.* New York: Basic Books.

Gleick, J. (1987). *Chaos: Making a new science.* New York: Viking Press.

Haley, J. (1976). *Problem Solving Therapy.* San Francisco, CA: Jossey Bass.

Heisenberg, W. (1962). *Physics and Philosophy: The revolution in modern physics.* New York: Harper & Row.

Heschel, A. J. (1951). *The Sabbath.* New York: Farrar, Straus and Giroux.

Heschel, A. J. (1965). *Who Is Man?* Stanford, CA: Stanford University Press.

Hillman, J. (1996). *The Soul's Code.* New York: Random House.

Hochschild, A. (1989). *The Second Shift: Working parents and the revolution at home.* New York: Viking Press.

Hofstadter, D. (1979). *Gödel, Escher, Bach: An eternal golden braid.* New York: Vintage Books.

James, W. (1902). The Confidences of a 'Psychical Researcher.' Essays in Psychical Research, *The Works of William James,* ed. Frederick H. Burkhardt. Cambridge, Mass: Harvard University Press, (1975-88).

Jaspers, K. (1951). *Way to Wisdom: An introduction to philosophy,* translated by Ralph Manheim. New Haven: Yale University Press.

Jung, C. G. (1921). *Collected Works,* Psychological Types. Vol. 6, London: Routledge and Kegan Paul.

Jung, C. G. (1959). *Collected Works,* The Structure and Dynamics of the Psyche. Vol. 8, Princeton, NJ: Princeton University Press.

Jung, C. G. (1961). *Memories, Dreams, Reflections.* New York: Random House.

Jung, C. G. (1971). *Collected Works,* Practice of Psychotherapy. Vol. 16, Princeton, NJ: Princeton University Press.

Keeney, B. (1983). *The Aesthetics of Change.* New York: The Guilford Press.

Kierkegaard, S. (1844). *The Concept of Anxiety.* Northvale, NJ: Princeton University Press, 1980.

Kierkegaard, S. (1849). *The Sickness Unto Death.* Northvale, NJ: Princeton University Press, 1980.

Klein, M. (1923). The role of the school in the libidinal development of the child. *The Writings of Melanie Klein,* Vol. 1. London: Hogarth Press.

Klein, M. (1929). Personification in the play of children. *The Writings of Melanie Klein,* Vol. 1. London: Hogarth Press.

Kohut, H. (1971). *The Analysis of the Self.* New York: International Universities Press.

Korzybski, A. (1933). *Science and Sanity: An introduction to non-Aristotelian systems and general semantic.* Englewood, NJ: Institute of General Semantics.

Laveman, L. & Borck, J. (1993). Relationship conflict resolution model: A short-term approach to couples counseling. *Family Therapy,* 20, (3), 143-164.

Laveman, L. (1997). The macrosystemic model of psychotherapy: Autonomy and attachment in family systems. *Journal of Psychotherapy Integration,* 7, (1), 55-74.

Levenson, E. (1972). *The Fallacy of Understanding: An inquiry into the changing structure of psychoanalysis.* New York: Basic Books.

Levi-Strauss, C. (1963). *Structural Anthropology.* New York: Basic Books.

Lorenz, E. N. (1994). *The Essence of Chaos.* University of Washington Press.

Machado, A. (1983). *Times Alone: Selected poems of Antonio Machado,* translated by R. Bly. Middletown, CT: Wesleyan University Press.

Mahler, M., Pine, F., & Bergman, A. (1975). *The Psychological Birth of the Infant: Symbiosis and individuation.* New York: Basic Books.

Mann, T. (1993). *Buddenbrooks: The decline of a family.* New York: Alfred A. Knopf.

Maslow, A. (1968). *Towards a Psychology of Being*. New York: Van Nostrand Reinhold.

May, R. (1950). *The Meaning of Anxiety*. US: The Ronald Press Company.

May, R. (1969). *Love and Will*. New York: W. W. Norton & Company.

McKee, M. (2003). Excavating our frames of mind: The key to dialogue and collaboration. *Social Work,* 48, (3), p. 401-408.

Merton, R. K. (1949). *Social Theory and Social Structure*. Glencoe: Free Press.

Musil, R. (1995). *The Man Without Qualities*. New York: Alfred A. Knopf.

Myers, G. (1986). *William James: His life and thought*. New Haven, CT: Yale University Press.

Myss, C. (1996). *Anatomy of the Spirit: The seven stages of power and healing*. New York: Harmony Books.

Neruda, P. (1993). "Nothing But Death," in *Neruda and Vallejo: Selected poems*, edited by Robert Bly. Boston, MA: Beacon Press.

Plato (1963a). "Meno", in *Plato: The Collected Dialogues,* Hamilton, E., & Huntington, C. eds., Bollingen Series 71. New York: Pantheon.

Plato (1963b). "The Republic", in *Plato: The Collected Dialogues,* Hamilton, E., & Huntington, C. eds., Bollingen Series 71. New York: Pantheon.

Roberts, M. (1996). *The Man Who Listens to Horses*. New York: Random House.

Selvini Palazzoli, M., Boscolo, L., Cecchin, G., & Prata, G. (1974). *Paradox and Counterparadox*. New York: Jason Aronson.

Singh, S. (1997). *Fermat's Enigma*. New York: Walker & Company.

Smith, H (1958). *The World's Religions*. San Francisco: HarperCollins.

Steinsaltz, A. (1998). *The Candle of God: Discourses in Chasidic thought*. Northvale, NJ: Jason Aronson.

Tan, A. (1989). *The Joy Luck Club*. New York: Putnam & Sons.

Tillich, P. (1999). *The Essential Tillich*. Chicago: The University of Chicago Press.

Twist, L. (2003). *The Soul of Money: Transforming your relationship with money and life*. New York: Norton.

Voegelin, E. (1957). *The World of the Polis*. Baton Rouge: Louisiana State University Press.

Wachtel, P. (1993). *Therapeutic Communication: Principles and effective practice.* New York: The Guilford Press.

Watzlawick, P. Beavin, J., & Jackson, D., (1967). *Pragmatics of Human Communication.* New York: W. W. Norton & Company.

Watzlawick, P., Weakland, J., & Fisch, R. (1974). *Change: Principles of problem formation and problem resolution.* New York: Norton.

Watzlawick, P. (1984). *The Invented Reality: How do we know what we believe we know?* New York: W. W. Norton & Company.

Welwood, J. (2000). *Toward a Psychology of Awakening: Buddhism, psychotherapy, and the path of spiritual transformation.* Boston: Shambhala.

Whitaker, C., & Napier, A. (1978). *The Family Crucible.* New York: Harper & Row.

Wilber, K. (1977). *The Spectrum of Consciousness.* Wheaton, Ill: Quest.

Wilber, K. (1995). *Sex, Ecology, and Spirituality: The spirit of evolution.* Boston, MA: Shambhala Publications.

Wilson, E. O. (1998). *Consilience: The unity of knowledge.* New York: Alfred A. Knopf.

Winnicott, A. (1945). *Primitive Emotional Development.* London, Tavistock, 1958.

Winnicott, A. (1951). *Transitional Objects and Transitional Phenomena.* London: Tavistock, 1958.

Winnicott, A. (1990). *Home Is Where We Start From. Essays from a Psychoanalyst.* New York: W.W. Norton & Company.

Wittgenstein, L. (1961). *Tractatus Logico-Philosophicus.* Translated by D. F. Pears and B. F. McGuinnes. London: Routledge & Kegan Paul.

Zukov, G. (1989). *The Seat of the Soul.* New York: Simon & Schuster.

Index

About the Author

Larry Laveman is Chief Clinical Director for Harmonium, a social service agency in San Diego, where he has been influential since 1980. In addition to overseeing clinical services and training licensed professionals in counseling methods, he maintains a private practice in Solana Beach, California, working with couples and adults. He has been a psychotherapist since 1975, having earned a master's degree in social work from Adelphi University. He is a Licensed Clinical Social Worker (LCSW) and a Board Certified Diplomate in Clinical Social Work. Striving to reach a larger audience of mental health professionals, he turned his attention to publishing in the early 1990s. His journal publications describe innovative models of therapy focusing on the integration of psychology and larger belief systems. *Mysticism and Modern Life* is his first book.

For more information
about Larry Laveman's approach to psychotherapy please visit:
www.larrylaveman.com

CPSIA information can be obtained
at www.ICGtesting.com
Printed in the USA
LV011951260721